UNSUNG

Thomas E. Carson

The Story of 10-Time
Gold Medal Olympic Champion
Ray Ewry

A 4/20 Publication   Copyright © 2017

DEDICATION

Throughout the last thirty-odd years, I have been so engrossed in this project that I might have seemed out of touch with the members of my family and close friends. I need to thank them for their patience and unwavering support.

To my wife, Cassandra, who has watched me enter my "writing cave" and disappear into the 1890s and early 1900s for over a decade, and to my loving sister, Jan, who shared Mary Elizabeth (Betsy) Ewry Carson's life and who has been totally supportive without ever seeing any of the drafts or pre-edited content, I give my utmost thanks.

Finally, to my sons, Thomas E. Carson VI and Adam Hunter Carson, and their wives, Cindy and Lori, of whom I am so very proud, I pass the Ray Ewry legacy on to them.

My deepest wish has always been to let them know who their great-grandfather was so they can, with Olympic pride, pass the family legacy down to my five amazing grandchildren:

Tommy, Phoebe, Dylan, Jake and Lily.

"Heaven is not reached at a single bound, but we build the ladder by which we rise from the lowly earth to the vaulted skies and we mount to its summit rung by rung."

Joshua Holland, 1831 – 1881

"The important thing in the Olympics is not to win but to take part: the important thing in life is not the triumph but the struggle."

Baron de Coubertin, 1896

NOTE FROM THE AUTHOR

The proper pronunciation of Ray's name is **"YOUR-REE"**

To keep the reader's costs down, the author decided to display the photographs and documents taken from Ray Ewry's archives in black and white.

If the reader wishes to view many more interesting black & white and color photographs along with legacy documents that grace this biography, please visit the **Facebook** page entitled **RAY C. EWRY**.

Should anyone wish to contact the author regarding more information on Ray Ewry, please feel free to contact:

Thomas E. Carson

carson.survivor17@gmail.com

ray.ewry.research.group@gmail.com

TABLE OF CONTENTS

Foreword by Bill Mallon, M.D.

Michael Phelps Recognition – Author

Regarding Citations – Author

CHAPTERS
PART ONE

PART TWO
THE PURDUE UNIVERSITY YEARS

AUTHOR'S INTRODUCTION TO PART THREE

PART THREE

THE OLYMPIC YEARS – 1900 – 1908

Foreword by Bill Mallon, M.D.

At the close of the 2008 Beijing Olympic Games, Michael Phelps had won 8 gold medals bringing his career Olympic medals total to 14: a new standard for Olympic brilliance. Phelps' feat was canonized by the world media, and they would often mention that he had broken the record of 9 Olympic gold medals jointly shared by Americans Carl Lewis, Mark Spitz, Finnish distance runner Paavo Nurmi, and Soviet gymnast Larisa Latynina.

There was little mention that one Olympian had won 10 gold medals at the Olympics, American jumper Ray Ewry, as his name had seemingly faded into obscurity. But hopefully, with this book, Tom Carson will reverse that fade. Ray Ewry competed over a century ago, in the Olympics of 1900, 1904, 1906, and 1908. It is those 1906 Olympics that had led to some of his oblivion.

Considered as Olympic Games at the time, they were special Games, as they did not fall into the standard every 4-year cycle, and over 40 years later the International Olympic Committee (IOC) decreed that they were not official Olympic Games. Ewry won 8 gold medals in 1900, 1904, and 1908, and the two additional that he won in 1906 brought his total to 10, but the IOC only recognizes the number as 8.

But the bulk of the world's Olympic historians consider the 1906 Olympic Games to be every bit as important, if not more so, than those of 1900 and 1904 and feel that Ewry's correct total should be 10.

This made him the leader for most Olympic gold medals won for over 100 years until Phelps bested him in Beijing.

Ray Ewry came to his Olympic glory in unusual circumstances. As a child, he suffered from polio and after he recovered, his doctor told him he needed to do physical exercise to overcome the effects of the disease. Ewry took up jumping exercises and specifically began competing in the standing jumps, which were only on the Olympic Program from 1900-to 1912.

He entered 10 Olympic events; the standing high jump, the standing long jump and the standing triple jump, and won every one of them. He is still considered the greatest ever exponent of the standing jumps, events which are now rarely held.

But still, there has never been a book-length biography of the man. Fortunately, Tom Carson has ended that grave omission. Tom is Ray Ewry's grandson and has collected information on his grandfather for many years. In the early 1990s, I spent a wonderful evening at Tom's home near Baltimore and he showed me all the memorabilia, medals, and trophies from Ewry's career. I am proud to still have a picture we took with what must be close to 100 such awards mounted on a stone wall in the backyard.

Because of the inside access, he has had to his grandfather's archives, Tom has been able to produce a wonderfully comprehensive look at his life and his career in athletics. It is written with the passion evident by someone honoring one of the greatest athletes of all time.

It is an inspiring story as we learn how Ewry overcame his childhood illness to win all those titles.

My gratitude goes out to Tom Carson for filling in this gap in the pantheon of biographies of great Olympic champions – in this case, one of the greatest of them all. Read it and learn and be inspired. You will be.

Bill Mallon, MD

Past-President and Co-Founder

International Society of Olympic Historians (ISOH)

IN THE COMPANY OF WORLD RECORD HOLDERS

Having known of Ray Ewry's Olympic achievements since I was a young boy, it was fascinating to look at Michael Phelps's run at the gold medal count in the 2004 Athens and the 2008 Beijing Games. He accumulated a total of nine individual gold medals from those Olympiads and at the end of the Beijing Games his gold medal count was 9 and his grand total was 16; two bronze and fourteen gold medals. Simply amazing!

I was born and raised in Baltimore, Maryland, and graduated from Towson High School in 1961. I was extremely proud of my fellow alum and knew back in 2008 that if Michael maintained the training regimen of his coach, Bob Bowman at the Meadowbrook Swimming Complex in Baltimore, he had a very good chance of equaling and breaking my grandfather's record of winning 10 individual Olympic gold medals when he participated in the 2012 London Olympics.

I remember seeing how humble long-time record-holders from various sports were on those special occasions when their records were broken, and I wondered how I would feel if my grandfather's 104-year-old record fell.

I had the absolute joy of watching my hometown hero, Cal Ripken, breaking Lou Gehrig's "Ironman" record of consecutive games as a Baltimore Oriole, and knew if Mr. Gehrig had been alive he would have delivered a humble and encouraging speech about the young baseball player who bested his long-held record.

I knew if Michael was successful in London, I would have to make that kind of speech to anyone who interviewed me. The old cliché, "records are made to be broken", would no doubt be uttered.

On August 2, 2012, Michael stood on his starting block ready to compete in the 200-meter individual medley final. I sat watching the race and knew that this might be the one that would tie Ray Ewry's record.

As Michael approached the wall I didn't know how I would feel. Would I be resentful…would I feel bitter that I could no longer brag about Ray Ewry's record?

When Michael touched the wall, I couldn't help myself. I leaped from my chair with a howl of joy. It wasn't thought out; it wasn't a forced emotion; it was the honest reaction to watching a true champion at his very best.

I had answered my own question when he tied Ray's record. All that was left was to wait until tomorrow to see if he would break it. To me, it was a foregone conclusion.

Again, Michael stood on the starting block for his signature event, the 100-meter butterfly, looking confident and ready.

At the 50-meter turn, I knew history would be re-written and Michael Phelps would earn his 11th individual Olympic gold medal and break the record held by the virtually unknown Olympian named Ray Ewry.

No longer could I, or anyone in my family, boast about Ray's long-standing record and I found that I was elated for Michael, his family, and the entire USA Olympic movement.

With Michael's final victory at the London Games, my resolve to share Ray Ewry's uplifting story strengthened and I went about the final editing of the biography that you see before you.

I must also congratulate Mr. Phelps on his amazing accomplishments at the 2016 Olympics in Rio.

His final medal count stands at 13 individual gold medals and a grand total of 28 Olympic gold medals.

It is with maximum respect for Michael Phelps, and all Olympians through the years, that I write this story of one unsung Olympic athlete who represents all that is good and sincere about those who challenge themselves to excel to greatness against all odds.

AUTHOR'S NOTE REGARDING CITATIONS

I wish to make it abundantly clear that various quotations and remembrances from, and references to Ray Ewry's personal letters, diaries, and journals will be found throughout this body of work.

These personal letters, diaries, and journals were the property of my mother, Mary Elizabeth Ewry Carson, Ray's only child, and were discovered in Baltimore in 1980. For over a year and a half, I constantly referred to them to absorb the rich history of my grandfather's life as a physically challenged young boy growing up in Lafayette, Indiana, and the years he spent as a student-athlete and Associate Professor at Purdue University in the 1890s.

Through the early 1900s after moving to New Jersey, his journals recorded his experiences as an inspector for the U.S. Navy and as the chief engineer for New York City's Naval Shipyard. His final journal was filled with his amazing accomplishments in four Olympic Games from 1900 through 1908.

Much of Ray Ewry's life after the Olympics is public domain information pertaining to his years working as a lead engineer for the New York Department of Water Supply.

Most of this segment of his life was portrayed through personal letters to his wife Nelle and articles in the New York Times regarding his work on the Catskills Project.

In the ancient tradition of handing down family history by word of mouth, my mother offered many hours of personal stories about her life in Douglaston, Long Island with Ray and Nelle.

Ray Ewry is an unsung athletic hero of the late 19th and early 20th century and it is with great pride that after the many years of research and joint discovery by a few dedicated people, I pieced together these elements to shed light on one of America's greatest early Olympians.

Thomas E. Carson V

Believe It Or Not — By Ripley

"AAAH"
THE FIRST WORD PRONOUNCED
BY A HUMAN BEING IS A TURKISH
WORD MEANING
"SUN"

WOTTA
DENTIST

J. B. WOTTA
IS A DENTIST
IN Kalamazoo, Mich.

RAY
EWRY
WORLD'S GREATEST JUMPER
WON
10
OLYMPIC
TITLES

PERSIAN CAT EATS CIGARETTES
AND CHEWING TOBACCO — REFUSES MILK.
Owned by MRS. EDW. McKEEN, W. Palm Beach, Fla.

1

GENESIS – Baltimore, Maryland – 1980

In November 1979, when I was in my mid-thirties, I returned to my hometown after decades of entertaining audiences as a rock and roll singer and later as a concert promoter for a resort nightclub. It was time to begin a new and uncharted chapter in my life. I had no job at that point and the pressure was on for me to jump back into the real world and find a career outside entertainment.

The new chapter I was looking for started one night in late December when I learned that the Soviet Union had invaded Afghanistan. I felt, as many Americans possibly did, that the invasion on the other side of the globe would not affect us. How wrong I was.

Our then President, Jimmy Carter, issued a threat to the Soviets regarding his total disdain for the invasion. Not wanting to initiate a military response, he came up with the strategy to use the United States Olympic team as a tool for leverage. Knowing the high level of competition between the U.S. and the Soviet Union, he figured he would boycott the Games of Moscow and their troops would withdraw shortly thereafter. The President had drawn a line in the sand.

He went on to declare that if by February 20th, 1980, the Soviet troops hadn't withdrawn from Afghanistan he would not allow the well-trained and eager U.S. Olympic Team to attend the Moscow Games.

I couldn't believe that such a threat would have any clout, knowing the Soviet's investment in the invasion. I kept thinking this was a ridiculous tactic.

After all the years of training and preparation, not to mention the cost, for Carter to ignore the hopes and dreams of so many athletes, their families, and their coaches would be selfish, and in fact, a very weak attempt at diplomatic pressure. Just before the February deadline, Carter chose Cyrus Vance to announce his intentions to the I.O.C. at the Winter Games in Lake Placid, N.Y.

Most of the athletes publicly protested the boycott and some even declared they would pay their own way to compete. Carter's response was to threaten to withdraw their passports. But he went one step farther from his "bully pulpit" by putting political pressure on many businesses sponsoring the Olympic movement.

The Soviets ignored his protest against the International, the United States Olympic Committee, and I am sure all the USA athletes, and the President went through with his boycott. For the first time since the Olympics started up again in 1896, the U.S. Olympic team was absent from the glorious spectacle.

It took the wind out of my sails and many millions of Americans as well. The only taste of the Olympics for us was the Olympic Boycott Games, which were called the "Liberty Bell Classic".

Since I lived so close to the University of Pennsylvania, I drove there and watched the competition between athletes from West Germany, Thailand, Kenya, Egypt, China and Sudan.

I thought the trip and the experience would buoy my spirits, but the experience only depressed me more.

With great satisfaction, I read that Renaldo Nehemiah's time of 13.31 seconds for the 110m hurdles was 8/10 ths of a second better than East Germany's Thomas Munkelt's time of 13.39 seconds.

My only solace was I could still watch the NBC coverage. I soon found out NBC's schedule went from 150 to less than a dozen hours. All I could see were snippets of events and occasional updates. My thirst for everything Olympic went unquenched.

On the last night of the Games, I watched a short segment of the closing ceremonies that pushed me to the bottom. I happened to glance at the picture above my desk of my grandfather, Ray Ewry, in his athletic garb.

I took the picture down and focused on his face and even deeper into his eyes.

As I stared, I thought I heard something like a whisper telling me to stop feeling sorry for myself, get off my butt, and do something about my life.

"The answer is right before you! You know what I've done and how I got there, so why don't you tell the world about me? After all, my history is part of you, and Betsy would know that you had kept your word to her."

Basically, it was like that great scene in "Moonstruck" when Cher slapped the guy and said, "Snap out of it!" The next morning, with a new sense of purpose, I began to conceive a plan to bring his story to print. I realized I had no real evidence of Ray's vast accomplishments other than a few of my mother's books on the Olympics.

But I remembered the belongings my mother had stored when she moved to South Carolina a few years ago to teach animal husbandry at Clemson.

I found the key to the storage unit she had entrusted me with, so I drove to the location and was escorted to the unit. Once inside the 10 x 20-foot unit, I began rooting through the dozens of sealed boxes of family items I hadn't seen in years.

My mother had been an avid reader and collector of books, many related to the Olympics. I packed as many boxes related to my grandfather and the Olympics as I could into my car and headed back to my apartment.

I began systematic cataloging of the items, laying old photographs in one pile, various letters in another, and documents in their own stack.

Finally, seeing only three weathered cardboard boxes remaining, and thinking I was near the end of my cataloging, I opened the first, labeled "Diaries and Journals", and discovered the mother lode.

Inside the box were two small diaries filled with Ray's juvenile handwriting. I was impressed that at the age of nine, he began to document his feelings and experiences. Under the diaries, I found five leather-bound, handwritten journals.

The first of these journals began in 1891 when my grandfather was a sophomore at Purdue University in West Lafayette, Indiana.

The last journal had been written in 1912.

For the next three weeks, I barely left my apartment. I read and re-read the diaries journals.

Thanks to his vivid recollections and exceptional writing style, I was transported back to a time when he experienced a life both terrifying and exciting.

With the thought of writing his story, I racked my memory trying to remember anything my mother had told me about her father, but I had been so young, and like most kids, I was only interested in what was going on around me.

Other than his scholarly portrait on our piano, more items linked to my grandfather were an old Purdue pennant and a framed hand-drawn map of Tippecanoe County, Indiana.

It portrayed existing cycling trails in the late 1800s that used to hang on my bedroom wall. The other items were a pair of authentic English longbows that had always been propped up against a wall in the garage.

ENGLISH LONGBOW © Public Domain

I recall one Saturday morning when my father had become rather upset at my keen interest in the longbows. He asked me to clean up the junk in the garage, but I got sidetracked, as young boys do sometimes.

I wanted to shoot some arrows in the woods later that day, but I found the bowstrings were old and rotten and snapped when I tried to move the loop up to the tip.

I had some money from my newspaper route, so I hopped on my bike and took off for the sporting goods store half a mile away.

I was supposed to be cutting the lawn after cleaning up the garage and being a super smart kid, I left the lawnmower running behind some bushes near the tree line at the far end of our spacious backyard.

I just knew the trick would work and Dad would think I was mowing.

When I got to the store I bought two of the longest bowstrings the man

had and rode like the wind back to the house.

Back in the garage, I set one looped end of the bowstring into the carved groove in the yellowed ivory tip, stepped between the bow and the string, and tried to bend the bow so I could set the other end of the string.

It was like trying to bend steel. I leaned the side of my thigh against the bow and pulled on the top with all my strength, but still…not an inch.

I relaxed and thought that sticking the bottom tip of the longbow into the finger hole of the sump pump cover might work, so I jammed it in and tried again.

For an instant, I thought the bow was bending, but as I struggled, I lost my balance and crashed into the wall. My father's tool pegboard wall came crashing down on me as his tools skittered across the garage floor. It sounded like an explosion. As I lay there, still clutching the longbow, I realized why the string would never work. It was a good eighteen inches short.

At that moment, my father barged into the garage, took one look at what I had done, and began yelling at me for abandoning my weekly grass cutting duty and destroying his prized tool pegboard.

My mother had also heard the commotion and seeing my leg stuck between the bow and the string and my father yelling at me, she immediately took command of the situation.

She calmed him down by getting me to promise to re-hang the pegboard, set the tools inside their corresponding outlines, and finish the yard.

"*It's always about your father,*" he said to her as he stormed back into the house. I had no idea what that meant. She explained that this was one of the cherished, hand-made Sherwood Forest English longbows from the 1800s. It had been presented to my grandfather by the Royals in 1908.

My mother assured me it would be a few years before I was strong enough to string them. I sure wish I had them now, but they were lost in all the moves my family made in the fifties and sixties.

When I told my father about my writing project he acknowledged my idea with a nod and then tactfully changed the subject.

I came to realize that my father held a deep and quiet resentment of Ray's international fame. I remember many times as a pre-teen when dragged to cocktail parties in the late fifties, my father would drift away from the group of people captivated by my mother as she enthusiastically told them Ray's story.

It's almost the same way my wife tends to engage other people at gatherings where I have a captured audience listening to my ramblings about my family's Olympian.

So now, I had Ray's personal record of his early childhood, his years at Purdue, and what led up to and through his involvement in the Olympics. With all this information, it was time to get to work.

Besides the few personal photographs, I realized there weren't many authentic photographs of his accomplishments other than the recurring pictures in all the Olympic reference books.

I began an intensive search through every vintage bookstore and bookstore chain along the eastern seaboard to see if I could find any photos I hadn't seen before but came up short.

With all the new documentaries coming to PBS and the BBC, I felt there had to be someone, or some research team, that might have discovered yet unseen material, be it still photographs or vintage film on the early Olympics or Ray Ewry.

Being an admirer of Jim McKay[1], the anchor for ABC's Wide World of Sports and the Olympic games, and knowing he was a Maryland native, I figured I'd try to tap into the best source I knew.

I called New York for information and asked for the sports department at ABC. I was directed to a receptionist who informed me that it would be impossible to talk to Mr. McKay as he was out of the country, but I could write him a letter. So, I did, knowing it might never reach him.

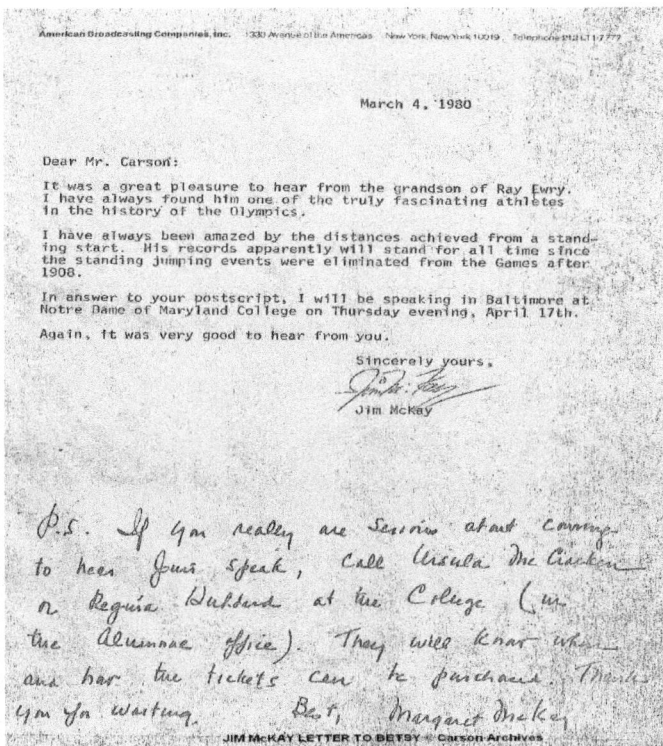

American Broadcasting Companies, Inc.   1330 Avenue of the Americas   New York, New York 10019   Telephone 212 LT 1-7777

March 4, 1980

Dear Mr. Carson:

It was a great pleasure to hear from the grandson of Ray Ewry. I have always found him one of the truly fascinating athletes in the history of the Olympics.

I have always been amazed by the distances achieved from a standing start. His records apparently will stand for all time since the standing jumping events were eliminated from the Games after 1908.

In answer to your postscript, I will be speaking in Baltimore at Notre Dame of Maryland College on Thursday evening, April 17th.

Again, it was very good to hear from you.

Sincerely yours,

Jim McKay

P.S. If you really are serious about coming to hear Jim speak, call Ursula McCusKen or Regina Hubbard at the College (in the Alumnae Office). They will know where and how the tickets can be purchased. Thanks you for waiting. Best, Margaret McKay

JIM McKAY LETTER TO BETSY • Carson Archives

---

[1] Jim McKay was the host for the 1960 Olympics on CBS-TV before moving to ABC.

When I received his response, I was ecstatic. I never thought that Mr. McKay would have the time to respond. This letter was the first evidence that some people knew of Ray Ewry, and to see the note by his wife Margaret made it so much more personal.

I called Notre Dame of Maryland and was told there were no tickets left. Since I lived only a few miles from the campus, I drove there and tried to wangle my way in, but to no avail.

It was the first roadblock in my discovery process. I knew there would be a few along the way, but I had no idea what kind or how many I would encounter. I was bound and determined to get started, and after all, I had to keep the promise I had made to my mother.

2

NEW YORK CITY – November - 1924

Trudging through the slush of a recent snowstorm, eighteen-year-old Tory Bliss approached the front door of the prestigious New York Athletic Club on Central Park South. He was a young man on a mission from Lafayette, Indiana.

His father, "Pup" Bliss, had convinced the administrators at Purdue University to fund a trip to New York so that a formal invitation to a very special event at the university could be hand-delivered by his son.

Tory asked the concierge if he could speak with Mr. Raymond Ewry and was told to take a seat in the spacious lobby. After a few minutes, a tall, lanky gentleman sat in the chair opposite Tory and introduced himself.

Somewhat nervous, Tory explained to Mr. Ewry that he was sent to formally invite him to the opening ceremony and dedication of a new sports facility at Purdue. Tory sat quietly as Mr. Ewry read the invitation.

To Alumnae Emeritus

Raymond Clarence Ewry

The Purdue Board of Athletics

Wishes to Extend the Invitation

To Be Keynote Speaker at the

Dedication and Grand Opening of

Ross - Aide Stadium

West Lafayette, Indiana

November 22, 1924

Over lunch, Tory implored his host to grant the wishes of his father and the Athletic Department at Purdue, and return with him to West Lafayette, Indiana for the ceremony, and at first, Mr. Ewry explained he was overwhelmed with his obligations to the New York City Water Department.

Tory was offered a room for the night and at breakfast the next day, Mr. Ewry informed him that he had done some re-arranging of his schedule and he would indeed be able to make the trip.

That evening, carrying his suitcase and an ornate wooden box, Mr. Ewry, and a very happy Tory Bliss boarded a westbound train. Once they settled into their Pullman cabin, Tory asked Mr. Ewry about the contents of the wooden box and was shown an antique urn.

The beautiful, meticulously painted figures on the urn depicted ancient Grecian athletes in different modes of athletic endeavor. One was throwing the javelin, another leaping over a high bar, a discus thrower, and an archer stood side by side and the last was a marathon runner in mid-stride.

There were two handles on opposite sides and a wax-sealed cap covered the opening at the top. When asked about the contents of the urn, Mr. Ewry told him he would have to wait until the ceremony for the answer.

The train was ahead of schedule, arriving an hour after sunrise. Once Ray had dropped his suitcase off at his hotel, he decided to look at his old residence in Lafayette.

After he saw the Elisha house, he walked around to the back and felt a twinge of melancholy upon seeing the small barn standing proudly in its state of disrepair.

Its exterior walls and roof were missing more than half the slats, the once traditional red paint had been sunbaked to a brown hue.

Emotions buried for over forty years began to surface. He had to reach back and activate long past mechanisms to suppress the unsettling memories.

He removed his glasses, took a deep breath, and approached the large double doors.

Before going through, he looked up to find the second-floor hay-baling door missing, but the large rusty winch wheel hanging from the four-by-four beam was still there.

He lifted the crossbar and struggled with the stubborn doors until they grudgingly gave way and he stood for a moment letting his eyes adjust to the deep shadows.

Shafts of sunlight streamed down from the sections of the missing roof, painting islands of light on the dirt floor. Dozens of barn swallows, disturbed by his entrance, flew high in the eaves and slipped out through the openings in the roof.

Every footfall caused dust to swirl around his shoes as he walked to a wheel-less carriage opposite the empty stalls in the barn. He removed his suit coat, hung it over the seat, and moved toward a large tarp-covered mound.

Gripping a corner, he slowly pulled the tarp to reveal two steel-banded, domed trunks.

Darker emotions washed over him as he spotted the top of an old wicker-backed chair partially hidden behind the trunks. A small wagon wheel rested on the arms of the chair. He dragged one of the trunks out to the open area.

With better light, he noticed the hastily painted name "EWRY" had chipped and faded with time. Eager to discover the contents, he went back to the pile and carefully pulled the antique chair free, and placed it next to the trunk.

His last task was to drag the second trunk over to the opening. By this time, he was perspiring. His clean white shirt was lightly coated with fine dust. He positioned the chair between the trunks and cautiously lowered his weight into the chair.

The wicker seat groaned but held fast, so he relaxed, leaned over to a trunk, unlatched the heavy brass clasp, and lifted the heavy, arched top.

Wrapped in faded red ribbons, stacks of journals and photographs slept under a thin layer of decades-old dust.

Untying a bundle of small journals, he began to read the top one that belonged to Mary Elisha and dated April 20, 1882.

"Dr. R. saw Ray again today. He had me boil water for the hot towels that he wraps around Ray's legs. I fear they scald the poor child. He used those God-awful long needles again too, but with no reaction. I must turn away as they are pushed into the knee joints.

Ray is such a brave boy. I wish poor Lizzie was still alive. She would be so proud of her son. I don't know how he can stand it day after day."

After a few moments of introspection, he closed the journal and reached into the chest for a faded envelope tied with a blue silk ribbon.

He gently opened the envelope to see two blue-tinted photographs. and smiled as he saw himself standing by his favorite bicycle. The second photo was of Nelle Johnson, the girl he was courting at that time.

Ray reached into a vest pocket, removed his handkerchief, and wiped the dust from his spectacles.

The unusually warm October afternoon and the rigors of the train trip had fatigued him somewhat and he leaned his head back again.

He held Nelle's picture up and thought about the day they had ridden their "wheels" out to the old Indian burial grounds in Tippecanoe County and used his new Eastman-Kodak "little black box" camera for the first time. He let his mind wander back through the years to a simpler time.

3

LAFAYETTE, INDIANA – The Early Years

Raymond Clarence Ewry was born on October 14, 1873, to George and Elizabeth "Lizzie" Ewry. George had been battling his dependence on alcohol for some time and allowed Lizzie to raise Ray. A few years later, she gave birth to Mabel just before she was diagnosed with consumption; known today as tuberculosis.

Ray's early years were no different than any other young boy growing up in Lafayette. Every day after school and every waking hour on the weekends, Ray would venture over to the woods that bordered the Wabash Canal and play games with his friends on the old towpath or head for the Tippecanoe battleground.

They loved to search for arrowheads and engage in the decades-old tradition of acting out the Battle of Tippecanoe where, in 1811, American forces had to do battle with Tecumseh, the mighty chief of the Shawnee tribe.

Lizzie's physical condition deteriorated quickly and by 1878 she was bed-ridden. On March 8, 1879, with Ray and Mabel being looked after by the neighboring Elisha's, Lizzie Ewry passed.

Recognizing that George would be incapable of raising his children, Mary Elisha demanded he move the children into their home, and soon after the children settled into life with the Elisha's, George left Lafayette.

No information has been found that relates to George's decision to leave Lafayette, but it is known that he traveled west. Many believed he wanted to get in on the thirty-year-old California gold rush.

Others thought that he too had come down with consumption and wanted to move to the drier climate of the southwest.

Opened in 1825, the grand old Wabash and Erie Canal was the conduit for commerce and news to thousands of people along the route from Lake Erie down to Evansville, Indiana, thus connecting it to the Ohio River.

For decades, it had been a valuable supply source and contributed greatly to the growth of the ever-expanding American frontier. But, with the rapid spread of rail construction, the canal's usefulness diminished.

In 1874, the canal was officially closed to government-sanctioned commercial barge traffic and by 1884 it had become no more than a slow-moving place for children to swim in. Small boats, canoes and a few privately-owned barges could be seen being pulled along the towpath or simply drifting slowly south. Some carried passengers while others ported small manifests of supplies, but most brought news from the big cities.

As it approached Lafayette, Indiana, the canal made a large bend at a place most of the local children called "the rocks". Grouped on the edge of the canal, large rocks formed an elevated platform.

A tight copse of trees surrounded the rocks with one thick branch extending above the largest rock where, years before, someone had attached a thick, knotted rope that dropped down to the top of the rock.

In young Ray's first journal, he described his favorite thing to do when playing with his friends at the "rocks" was to try and swing out over the canal just like an old canal barge captained by a retired English sea captain with the old English name of Spigot passed by the rocks.

There was always stiff competition among the boys to land squarely on the small grass patch in the stern of the barge that offered food to the two "pull" mules that Captain Spigot kept on board for towing in slow-moving sections of the canal.

On blistering, hot summer days, many of the children in Lafayette found the only escape from the heat was a cool dip in the canal. As a sweet payoff, any adventurous boy who accomplished the tricky timing of his swing and landed on the patch would receive a handful of hard candy.

The scandal of the incoming trains dumping human waste into the Wabash had been publicized in both local papers.

Parents forbade their children to swim in the canal. But, as all parents know, boys will be boys. It didn't help matters that many cowherd foremen, to save time, had opted to forego the long trek to the crossover bridges into Lafayette by making their herds cross the narrow shallow sections of the canal, adding bovine fecal matter to the human waste in the water.

It wasn't until after the evidence of widespread paralysis had infected dozens of Lafayette children the powers that be prohibited the trains from dumping waste and cattlemen were directed to use alternate bridges for cattle crossings.

One such morning in late June found Ray and his pals had come to the towpath next to the canal to play their favorite game, "Foot-an'-Half"[2].

After the boys were soaked with sweat and covered in towpath grime, they would undress and plunge headlong into the slow-moving Wabash.

Little did the boys know that lurking in the tranquil canal waters was a bacterium that would change many lives in Lafayette, Indiana.

Tippecanoe County Fairgrounds – July 4, 1881

People began to gather before sunrise for the eight o'clock opening of the gates to the fairgrounds. This was the annual three-day County Fair holiday celebration and when the gates opened, hundreds of people filtered onto the fairgrounds where they came to spend time relaxing, eating foods from the various vendors. Most looked forward to cheering for and betting on the different jockeys dressed in colorful silks in the various horse races.

Many family-oriented events were scheduled for each afternoon and at the end of each day, just after sundown, everyone wandered around to the northeast corner of the fairgrounds to watch the fireworks.

---

[2] Found in the book "Dan Beard's Games"

The perimeter of the fairgrounds was dotted with exhibition corrals for the various livestock competitions, while tented booths lined both sides of the midway.

Merchants from Lafayette and neighboring counties extolled the value and quality of their goods along with hucksters offering games of chance.

Earlier in the week, the County Fair committee had volunteers trim an oval track in the southwestern corner of the grounds and erect wooden viewing stands for over two hundred people at the finish line.

At 9 AM, the end of wagering bell rang for the first horse race. Moments later, using the customary shotgun start, the first of ten daily horse races began.

At 11 AM, in a far corner of the fairgrounds, twenty boys lined up to have numbered clothes pinned to their shirts.

These were the young competitors for the yearly "Great Wheelbarrow Frog Race of Tippecanoe County".

For the children of Lafayette and surrounding towns, this was the biggest thing in their lives. Each year, one of the wealthier landowners would award the winner the newest foal from his horse stables. To be a youngster and own your horse was everything.

After getting his race number, Ray joined his friend "Pup" in the race preparation area where they huddled around a flatbed wooden wheelbarrow.

When beckoned, all the competitors stood in front of the stage as the Master of Ceremonies opened his arms to the crowd and explained the rules for the day's race. Each boy had to place their frog on the wheelbarrow and set the wheel on the start line.

At the sound of the gun, they were to push their wheelbarrow over the half-mile course making sure to stay within the ropes on either side.

If any frog left a wheelbarrow, the boy had to collect the frog and place it back before they could proceed. The first boy to cross the finish line here would win the foal.

Twenty brightly painted wheelbarrows were lined up on the start line. Each boy gripped the handles tightly and waited for the starting shotgun blast. When the shotgun fired, eight frogs immediately leaped off their barrows. The crowd at the start line burst into laughter and jeers as the boys lunged after their frogs.

Ray's frog was fat and heavy, and it stayed on the wheelbarrow, so he exploded off the start line with the other six boys.

With his size and strength, he moved out in front. As the pack of boys raced across the flat, grassy field toward the woods, the most aggressive ones aimed their wheelbarrows directly at others.

This caused numerous collisions where fights broke out and frogs went flying in the air as the spectators roared their approval.

Ray was hit twice by older competitors but only had to chase his frog once. He allowed the older boys to pass him, opting to slip to the rear of the violent pack and stay safe. He knew that there would be more collisions in the woods, so he kept his eyes on the trail. The key was not to hit anything that would jar the wheelbarrow and as the trail narrowed near the woods, Ray was in sixth place.

Once it meandered through the woods, the trail connected to the towpath next to the canal.

As Ray left the woods he saw two boys who had been pushed into the canal struggling to grab their wheelbarrows before they floated downstream.

At the halfway point, Ray was moving along confidently as he veered back into the woods.

This was when he began to feel a tingling in his feet for the first time. He ignored the feeling and kept churning his legs up a slight incline.

Farther up the wooded trail, while Pully was trying to knock another boy out of the race, he hit a rock and his wheel shattered and his frog flew into the air, landing in some brush beside the trail. He searched frantically, finally finding it under a log.

Running back to his battered wheelbarrow, he heard someone coming up the trail. He saw Ray coming on fast and crouched behind a large tree and stuffed his frog into a pants pocket.

Ray slowed as Pully's useless wheelbarrow came into view. He scanned the trees on both sides of the trail but saw nothing.

Suddenly, hands grabbed his shoulders from behind and threw him to the ground as the wheelbarrow tilted and dislodged his frog.

As Pully grabbed Ray's wheelbarrow and headed off up the trail toward the open field for the final leg of the race, Ray spotted his frog. He grabbed it and started running after Pully.

At the wood's edge, when Ray saw Pully put his frog on his wheelbarrow and start across the open field toward the finish line, he pushed himself harder, trying to close the gap.

As he reached the flat open section, his legs began to feel oddly heavy. The same tingling feeling began to creep up from his feet. With each footfall, his ability to keep moving diminished.

Behind the finish line, Pup watched Ray falling farther behind Pully. Mary Elisha and Mabel stood next to him watching Ray waiver and then stumble. They gasped as he got up and began to run again.

He got within fifty yards of the finish and fell hard this time. As some of the spectators started pointing at the struggling boy out in the field, Pup broke from the spectators and ran to Ray.

He stayed with him until the race ended and watched as men lifted young Ray into a buckboard and drove him to Elisha's house.

Candlelight bathed Ray's bedroom as Mary Elisha and Dr. Harvey Rainey stood next to the bed wrapping steaming towels around Ray's legs.

After a few minutes, Dr. Rainey removed the towels and, to the young boy's horror, withdrew a long slender steel needle from his black bag.

Ray wrote that Dr. Rainey was less than gentle and the sight of the long needle penetrating the skin around his knees and ankles to determine nerve responses frightened him.

After a few sessions, Mary Elisha demanded that the practice is stopped.

She wondered just how much pain the young boy could endure and wept for Ray and little Mabel when she thought about the abandonment of the children by their father.

Add to that the long-suffering from consumption by their mother, Lizzie, and finally, her death when Ray was only six years old.

Dr. Rainey stopped the needles but continued to come by every other week to check in on Ray. After each visit, Dr. Rainey would encourage Mary Elisha to continue wrapping the steaming hot towels around his legs.

After eight months of this routine, he finally told Mary Elisha that the paralysis had stopped its ascending manner, but there was nothing else he could do for the boy.

Ray's legs were useless, and the sad fact was that he would have to face his future from his bed. Mary Elisha became very upset with Dr. Rainey and refused to accept his final prognosis.

She asked if there might be someone else with more information on Ray's illness who could be contacted and mentioned that the cost was of no consequence to her.

Dr. Rainey informed her that he did have a colleague at the newly constructed Johns Hopkins hospital in Baltimore, Maryland and that he would telegraph him to inquire about assistance.

4

LAFAYETTE, INDIANA - 1885

What would have been a customary Christmas morning was overshadowed by young Ray's illness. Mary Elisha did the best she could by adorning the house with the standard seasonal decorations, but they did little to boost the depression Ray was falling into.

Ray wrote that on that Christmas day, after crawling to the chair by his bedroom window and seeing his friends playing in the snow, he became very bitter. He stayed in his upstairs room refusing to allow anyone to carry him down to open presents and enjoy the large breakfast Mary Elisha had prepared.

When Captain Spigot, the barge master, arrived with presents for the family, Ray still refused to come down to meet his old friend. Finally, the Captain went to Ray's room with a large rectangular box.

When Ray's reluctance to open, the box became evident, the Captain ripped it open to reveal a pair of new, wooden crutches. The Captain was surprised when Ray knocked the box to the floor and screamed that he didn't want any presents. He explained that the crutches would allow him to get out and about, but a solemn Ray told him that he would never walk again.

The Captain tried in vain to convince him to be positive and have hope, but Ray simply refused to talk and demanded to be left alone, so the Captain set the crutches next to Ray's bed and left him to deal with one of his first challenges.

A few days later, Dr. Rainey stopped by to inform Mary Elisha that he had sent a wire to a colleague who was working in the new Johns Hopkins hospital in Baltimore.

A week later, he received a return message that there were new and exciting advances in physical therapy and that he would inquire further.

Two weeks after that, Dr. Rainey was informed that a trained specialist who had achieved notable success with experimental exercises would be coming to Indiana for some medical forums and would be calling on Mary Elisha once prior obligations were completed.

Baltimore - 1980

Having read through the entire set of journals for the first time, I wondered if there might be any memorabilia I had missed. I returned to the storage unit and began rummaging through the remaining boxes.

I came across one box filled with notebooks and folders containing letters addressed to my grandmother. I decided to pack the remaining unmarked boxes in the car and drove back to my overly crowded room.

Later that night, I found a small metal box with a rusted snap-lock. It took a pair of pliers to pry the top off and to my delight, I came across a small silver bracelet with eight nautical flag squares separated by an emblem of what seemed to be a foot with a wing attached to it.

I recalled Ray had written about a winged foot and the New York Athletic Club, which he joined around the turn of the century. Here was another New York connection I knew had to be investigated.

On September 8th, 1868, three gentlemen athletes, Mr. Buermeyer, Mr. Babcock, and Mr. Curtis along with eleven other sportsmen met in a Manhattan tavern known as the Knickerbocker Cottage.

This meeting turned out to be the first gathering of the New York Athletic Club. Their mission was collectively focused on developing and improving the amateur sports venue and establishing a method to make all event measurements uniform.

Since that day, the NYAC has steadily grown and prestige to become one of the foremost Athletic Clubs in the United States, if not the world. I was thoroughly impressed with the history of this venerable establishment and was anxious to talk to people who represented amateur sports at such a high level.

Imagine my excitement when I found an original poster of the founders during my research on the web and saw the same "winged foot" on the flag. I had hit pay dirt.

So, I called information again. When I reached the operator at the Club, she forwarded my call to the Executive Secretary, Mr. Victor Willman. Mr. Willman was polite but seemed a bit nervous after I introduced myself as the grandson of Ray Ewry.

He was a practiced professional, taking my name, address and phone number and he informed me that my identity would have to be verified.

He said the Club was very protective of their member's personal information and someone would be in touch with me regarding my inquiries within a few days.

Before I let him go, I asked if the words "winged foot" meant anything to him. He answered in a mildly condescending manner.

"Why of course, young man!"

"It's our iconic image of the foot of a Grecian athlete strapped in a sandal. It happens to be the emblem used by the NYAC on their stationary. All athletic garb is worn by the athletes representing the Club in the competition. It is also the name of our Club magazine."

Encouraged by the new information, I went to my Encyclopedia Britannica and looked up the nautical flag alphabet, and matched the flag squares on the bracelet to the corresponding letters. It was obviously my mother's...a gift from her father. The translation of the nautical flags was:

B E T Z   E W R Y

One thing that had me a bit curious was why my identity had to be confirmed. I finally agreed that they were proper in doing so, as any Tom, Dick, or Harry could simply state they were related to a member of the NYAC and get private information, and after all, my last name was Carson, not Ewry.

Even though I had told Mr. Willman I was Ray's grandson, I was naïve enough not to mention that my mother was Ray's only child. I realized that I was stepping into unfamiliar territory and had better learn the rules of engagement.

I began to catalog all the items I had found in the various boxes and once I had emptied them all, I realized that there was no sign of any Olympic memorabilia. Mom had spoken of Ray being in the Olympics many times and yet there were no tangible items in her archives. So, I added another question to my growing list.

"Where are the gold medals?"

A week later, I had not heard from anyone from the New York Athletic Club, so I called the Club and was immediately connected with Mr. Willman again. He apologized for not calling, telling me how busy they were.

This time, though, I informed him that whoever was checking out my identity should know that Mom's maiden name was Ewry and if necessary, I could fax him a copy of her birth certificate, as well as mine.

I also told him that I might be coming to New York soon with a good friend, Leo D'Aleo, a talented and much-heralded architect here in Baltimore.

Leo had won numerous awards for his refurbishing of the Baltimore City Hall. New York City's Mayor Koch had seen what he had done in Baltimore and invited Leo to New York to be considered by a committee to do the same for the City Hall of New York.

Again, I sensed a curious level of nervousness from Mr. Willman. He said that once I had a concrete date I should call ahead, and he would be honored to let Leo and I stay, carte blanche, at the Club while in New York.

He concluded the conversation by telling me that he would confer with the Executive Director, Mr. Reddington, regarding a possible meeting while I stayed at the Club.

Quietly, my instinctual alarm bells began to sound. Why would I be afforded a free stay at such an exclusive club, and a meeting with the Director, if they hadn't had the time to check and confirm my identity regarding my claim of being Ray's grandson?

I had no idea that shortly I would experience a tragic and deeply disturbing revelation regarding a 1978 incident at the Club.

5

LAFAYETTE, INDIANA – 1886

Mary Elisha was a strict woman, and when it came time for Ray to resume his studies, she arranged with Mrs. Johnson, a teacher at Jefferson-Centennial school, to have the required books and lesson plans brought to her house.

Once a week, Mrs. Johnson would drop off the "homework" she wanted Ray to complete. This routine lasted for the entire school year and in June, Ray was notified that, even though he was tutored at home, he was in the top 10% of his class, excelling in mathematics and art.

A few weeks after school started, Mrs. Johnson and her young daughter, Nelle, came out to the house to take Ray on a pre-arranged outing. They were driven by Elisha's helper, Ben, to the center of Lafayette where Mrs. Johnson gave Ray a set of drawing "leads", pencils in our modern parlance, and a blank page drawing book.

Ray wrote of his awkwardness when Mrs. Johnson left him and Nelle to themselves. He never spoke to her on that day. Rather than have a conversation with the younger girl, he began to sketch the courthouse and many of the buildings being erected in the center city.

When Mrs. Johnson dropped Ray off at home, she showed Mary Elisha the sketches and told her that Ray was very talented and that they should gear his education toward college. Mary Elisha recognized this as a breakthrough and encouraged Ray to develop his drawing talents.

When Captain Spigot arrived with supplies for Elisha's general store, he gave young Ray a copy of Pulitzer's "The World" newspaper. Mr. Pulitzer petitioned citizens to contribute any monies they could spare to a special fund to pay for the pedestal.

The new gift from the French, the Statue of Liberty, needed a strong foundation for it to be displayed safely.

When Ray saw the hand-drawn statue on the front page, he began to copy the image repeatedly.

On any given morning, Mary Elisha would enter his bedroom and find dozens of discarded sheets of paper with Ray's depiction of the massive bronze structure. Seeing his keen interest in the Statue of Liberty, Mary Elisha introduced Ray to a section of baling wire and a wooden tub of plaster of Paris.

At first, Ray wasn't interested in the raw materials sitting in the corner of his bedroom, but within a week he began to create his statue from scratch.

Once he began creating a mock-up of the statue, Mary Elisha had to implement a strict schedule that allowed Ray to engage in his project only after his studies were complete.

Within a month, she saw a marked difference in his overall attitude. He wasn't complaining as much about being sequestered in his bedroom while all his friends were enjoying the outdoor games he used to play. With each visit, Mrs. Johnson was asked to bring any books or newspapers that had anything related to the new statue in New York.

In late July, Captain Spigot's barge meandered south on the Wabash with his usual manifest of supplies for his clients along the waterway, including five barrels of molasses, dozens of containers of spices, and over a dozen bolts of material for Mary Elisha's general store. Throughout his time on the Wabash, the Captain had ported hundreds of trappers, gold miners and families on their way west, but on this particular trip, the Captain allowed a solitary passenger to pay for the journey "down canal" as they used to say.

Captain Spigot had never allowed a single female on the barge, but because she told him that she was seeking a certain Dr. Rainey and the Ewry family,

During her initial meeting with Dr. Rainey, she was told of Ray's issues and the various archaic methods used to possibly counter the effects of the paralysis. She was horrified.

Once the meeting was over, she was taken to the Elisha's to meet the family and hopefully establish a successful regimen of therapy for young Ray.

In Ray's journals, the name Kate was mentioned many times, sometimes referring to her as Doctor Kate. Other than his journal accounts there are no other references to this woman, but it became evident early on that this woman was the key to his rehabilitation.

Ray noted the first thing she did was promise to never use needles to test his nerves or use the scalding towel wraps that he hated so much. Her approach was more of muscular stimulation and long, deep muscle massage therapy. Once Kate had secured young Ray's trust, she began an ongoing search for ways to get Ray to leave his room and get outside.

Her first idea came from her memories of the way hospitals back east erected long, round, metal tubes to be used as fire escape chutes.

They were erected under the designated "end of hall" windows on each floor. The chutes sloped down and away from the buildings and ended on the ground safely out of harm's way.

When Kate told Mary Elisha of her plans to get Ray out of his room, Mary Elisha would have to speak to her free slave Benjamin.
Known to everyone as Ben, he was temporarily relieved of his duties at the store and asked to assist Kate.

Kate had seen some old wooden barrels in the small barn and thought they would make a good escape chute if they could be secured together and placed on some kind of ramp. It took Kate and Ben more than two weeks to cut and strip the long narrow trees needed to create the chute.

Ray wrote that to raise the trees up to his second-floor bedroom window, Ben had tied a rope to the end of a tree, tossed it to Kate who was hanging out of his window, looped it around one of Ray's bed's legs, and threw it back down to Ben.

Ben would climb up on Mary Elisha's horse, loop the rope around the horn of the saddle, and back away from the house so that the rope pulled the end of the tree up to the window where Kate fastened it to the legs of a heavy dresser.

Once the trees had been lifted, Kate and Ben rolled out the barrels from the barn and knocked out the bottoms.

He then lined them up in a row and lashed them so that the first barrel sat at the base of the trees. It took a few times of trying to pull the barrels up the tree poles. Their biggest fear was the possibility that the weight of the barrels might splinter the poles.

Once Ben had cut down some shorter trees and used them to prop up the two long trees angling up to Ray's window.

The rope was attached to the lead barrel, and the other end was looped around the bedpost again and tossed down to Ben who sat on Firefly.
It was a triumphant moment when the barrels slowly moved up the track and bumped against the bedroom windowsill.

Ray noted that at the time, he firmly believed Kate's plan was a total waste of time.

Once the barrels were secured, both Kate and Ben had to prove to Ray that it was safe by sitting on flat burlap seed bags and sliding down the chute to the backyard.

As Mary Elisha watched near the base of the chute, Ray slid down to the backyard for the first time. It was a short ride, but once Ray found that his world could change, he became very enthusiastic about the idea of escaping his bedroom and finally feeling the sun on his face.

This was the first step for young Ray. Kate had proved to him that things could be done to improve his life without causing him pain and he began to trust her.

And so, Ray's journey into the world of physical rehabilitation began. Kate warned him that it would not be easy, but if he believed not only in her but also in himself, his life just might change forever.

When Ray proved he could move over to the window and lift himself up and into the mouth of the chute, the next stage in his physical therapy began.

Kate had noticed the heavy beam jutting out above the bail door of the barn and the rope dangling to the ground from the winch wheel.

Again, she ventured inside the barn looking for things to create some kind of apparatus that would advance Ray's rehab. She found a heavy peach basket resting on a rack of leather straps and the germ of an idea blossomed.

Four holes were cut under the thick reinforced rim of the basket and leather straps were looped through and tied in a tight knot. The other ends of the straps were tied in a single knot and secured the winch rope to the knot.

Next, an old layered plate spring was pulled from a pile of discarded buggy parts.

The spring was anchored to the ground some twenty feet from the basket. Kate tied knots every twelve inches or so on the loose end of the rope and looped it under the middle of the arched spring. She could pull on the rope and the basket would move up and down easily.

Once Ray had slipped down the chute and landed in the soft hay at the base, Ben and Kate carried him over and slipped his useless legs through the holes in the basket.

Ben moved to the spring end of the rope and began to pull. The basket lifted, and Ray's legs dangled straight down, his toes barely touching the ground.

Kate instructed Ben to lower the basket until Ray's feet were flat on the grass with his knees bent at a 90-degree angle. Ben tied the end of the rope into a knot to keep Ray's legs at that exact angle. Kate walked over to Ray and urged him to push down with his legs and try to lift the basket.

For the next hour, Ray tried his best, but the result was an angry, sweat-soaked boy who became upset that nothing happened. All the encouragement from Kate and Ben was wasted on him as he began to throw a temper tantrum and demanded to be taken to his room.

After that first attempt in the basket, every morning for three weeks Kate would go to Ray's room and suggest he try the chute and basket again, but he would refuse the offer and go back to working on his Statue of Liberty model.

A few days later, Ben came to the house with a set of steps he found in the storage room of the store and placed them next to the basket. He explained to Kate that if left alone, Ray's curiosity might compel him to slide down the chute, crawl across the short distance to the steps and somehow figure out how to get up the three steps and climb into the basket.

She couldn't figure out why he was so against working with her until one day she asked him to give her one concrete reason why he was against exercising. He told her that he was thirteen and felt he shouldn't have to rely on other people.

On a warm night in October, Mary Elisha, Kate, and Ben sat on the small back porch after another day of looking at the unused peach basket hanging there in the yard.

Kate was thumbing through the catalog when she came to the section on medical assistance items and saw a fancy and very expensive wheelchair.

She turned the catalog around so the other two could see it and watched as Ben jumped up, grabbed a lantern, excused himself, and disappeared into the barn.

In the morning, Kate began the daily routine of lifting Ray into the chute and going into the backyard to get Ray as he came out of the chute, but this particular morning was different.

As Ray and Kate met at the base of the chute, they saw a high-back cane chair with a wooden wheel on each side. Ben had attached a metal rod to act as the spoke and two wheels to make Ray his hand-made wheelchair. Kate lifted him into the chair and watched as he enthusiastically pushed on the wheels and rolled over to the steps.

Later that night, Ray confided in Kate that what he hated the most was the crawling. Crawling to the window in his bedroom was bad enough but having to crawl across the backyard was embarrassing.

This is when Kate told Ray that the crawling across the yard was connected to his rehabilitation. She explained that for Ray to become independent, he would have to build his upper body strength. Crawling would help to build his chest and arm muscles so he could lift himself into the basket.

Kate had to travel to Indianapolis for a few days to attend a conference of therapists at one of the hospitals. Upon her return, she came into the Elisha house and found no one home.

She went into the kitchen and through the window saw Ray and his friend Pup, trying to get him to the basket. It took everything Pup had to lift his lanky friend over the edge of the basket and slip his legs through the holes, but he finally did it.

The next thing Kate saw astounded her. Pup got on his hands and knees under the basket and while urging Ray to push with his legs, he arched his back and made the basket lift.

Whether Ray believed that he raised the basket on his own or with Pup's help, it made an impression on him and he was overjoyed with his success.

After that day, Pup would come by and help Ray over to the mouth of the chute and the two of them would sit on the burlap bag, slide down, crash into the hay bale, and roll in the grass laughing.

Over the next month, with the encouragement from Pup, Ben, and Kate, Ray began to lift the basket by himself. It was only an inch or two in the beginning, but young Ray had latched on to a steady regimen of exercising with the basket every morning, resting through midday and exercising most of the afternoon until he slumped in the basket, totally exhausted. What Ray didn't realize was the fact that the basket would be lowered a few times each week, so he would have to exert more pressure with his lifts.

When Kate saw Ray finally enjoying himself, she knew it was time to move forward, so the next time Captain Spigot delivered supplies for the store, he helped her order something very special for Ray.

Captain Spigot promised Kate that he would bring the item on his next trip down the canal.

Kate knew it might take two to three weeks for Captain Spigot's turn-around, so she began to have three-a-day sessions for Ray to exercise. Each was shorter in length but more intense for Ray. After the first week, he was lifting the basket more than six inches. He was gaining muscle mass and strength and his resolve to make it to a standing position grew each day.

On his birthday, he gave Mary Elisha, Ben, and Kate a present by calling them all out into the yard. He wrote that he had climbed into the basket by himself, waited for them to surround him, and proceeded to take a deep breath, push down with his feet and lift the basket to the point where he was standing.

Later that day, Captain Spigot arrived with his regular supplies for the store and a rectangular box for Ray.

It was time for the third session of the day, so Ray slid down the chute, climbed into the makeshift wheelchair, rolled over to the steps, and climbed into the basket.

The Captain stood and watched in amazement as Ray pressed his shoes into the grass and lifted the basket until he was standing tall in front of him.

After watching the boy's effort, the Captain went to the large rectangular box, opened it, and handed Ray a pair of polished wooden crutches. When Kate demonstrated how he was to use them, Ray wanted to abandon the basket and try the crutches.

The Captain told him to wait and went back to the box and pulled out what would change Ray's life forever. Kate lifted him from the basket and strapped on a shiny metal and leather set of braces she had ordered weeks before. Next, Ray placed the crutches under his arms and stood free of human assistance for the first time.

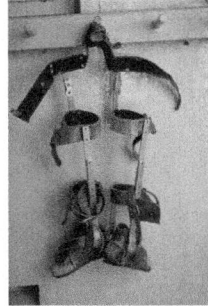

This moment sparked something that stayed with him for the rest of his life. He realized determination and the will to succeed no matter what the challenge would be with him for the rest of his life.

The sight of Ray walking with his crutches and braces signaled a new chapter in his rehabilitation. The days of laboring in the peach basket were over, and Ray was growing like a weed and couldn't fit into it anymore.

Ben had built a bench for Ray to rest on and erected two tree limbs three feet apart that forked at Ray's shoulder level. Next, a four-foot stripped birch limb had notches cut in at either end to accommodate the rope loops of old burlap seed bags filled with dirt.

Kate would place the limb across Ray's shoulders and hang the seed bags onto both ends. With his braces firmly strapped to his waist and legs, Ray would begin his day with the lightest bags and squat down until his thighs were parallel to the ground, hold for a few moments, then push down with his legs until he was upright again. The weights were increased until his legs began to shake.

Kate had been keeping a record of Ray's achievements in her journal from the first day she arrived. It was almost full after the months she had been working with him. Each day had been noted whether he exercised or not. Early on, Kate had noticed that Ray was growing quickly and on the first of each week, she would prop him up against his bedroom door jam and mark it.

Since her arrival in Lafayette, Ray had grown eight inches and was approaching five feet eight inches. Since Ray was only thirteen, she knew he would grow to be much taller than most men since the average adult male was around five feet seven.

One day, after watching Ray come down the stairs with just the aid of his braces, walk through the house, and out into the backyard to begin his squatting drills, she realized there was nothing more she could do for him.

He was on his way and she knew nothing would stop him until he was back to walking as he did before the paralysis started. It was time to go.

When Kate told everyone that she would be going home, it was like a member of the family was leaving. Ray was extremely sad to hear the news. After a long walk down by the canal, and a heartfelt explanation as to her reasons, he realized she had accomplished what she had come to Lafayette for.

6

NEW YORK CITY - 1980

When I arrived in New York City, I was extremely excited. I had only visited the city a few times during my rock and roll years and any memories of those times were simply a blur. The first thing I saw was a long awning jutting out over the sidewalk from above the front door and the huge columns, one with a declarative brass plaque.

Upon entering the Club, one would think it to be the lobby of a five-star hotel. It was enormous. You could feel the history of the place envelope you. I was welcomed by the concierge and after confirming our reservations, he handed me a sealed envelope from Mr. Willman. It was a formal note of welcome. It also informed me that I had a meeting arranged with Mr. Reddington the next day at 11:00 am in the executive offices upstairs.

After settling in, I went down to the first floor to do some scouting and afterward, went into the dining hall for lunch. As I stood at the entrance, waiting to be seated, men in suits, coats, and ties were looking at me strangely.

I realized my social *faux pas* when, without a word, I was handed a blue blazer and a clip-on stripped Club tie. After lunch, I went back to the room and read the welcome kit that told of an Olympic-sized swimming pool in the building. Perfect! There's nothing like a relaxing dip in the pool, right? I must admit that I was somewhat surprised to see most of the men sitting around and swimming in the pool were "au natural". That's when I realized the old traditions were an integral part of the New York Athletic Club.

The next morning, I began reading a hardback copy of the history of the NYAC. I wanted to be informed about the Club when I met with Mr. Reddington.

Ten minutes before the meeting, I took the elevator to the Executive Offices and sat in the anteroom with the receptionist and waited...and waited...and waited.

Finally, forty minutes past the appointed time, I asked the receptionist to contact Mr. Willman. After another twenty minutes, Mr. Willman came out of his office and motioned for me to come in. I sat across from his desk, somewhat irritated but thankful that something was happening.

He sat down and opened a folder on his desk and read for a few seconds before looking up at me with what I perceived as his "corporate" smile. He asked me how I liked the accommodations at the Club as he presented me with the newest edition of the rich history of the New York Athletic Club.

I thanked him for the book and expressed my appreciation for the room and the fabulous meal I enjoyed the night before. When he finally asked the reason for my trip to New York, I told him that I was here to collect the medals and trophies that my mother had loaned the Club after her father's death in 1937.

He told me it might take some time and that today was a busy day at the Club and the best thing might be to allow him some time to gather all Ray's memorabilia. This was not what I wanted to hear, but I had no choice but to go along with his suggestion that I return home and wait for the Club to mail the items to me.

I asked Mr. Willman if I could at least take Ray's gold medals home with me.

It was at that moment that his demeanor changed. Talk about getting ominous vibes from someone sitting before you.

He looked down at his hands as he told me that in 1978 someone had entered the Club, slipped past the lobby guard, and removed all the gold medals. At that moment, it felt like all the oxygen left the room.

I broke out in a cold sweat and a growing rage began boiling up from within. For a moment, I was speechless. I guess Mr. Willman saw my shock and disappointment.

I felt as if someone had hit me with a truck. The room began to close in on me. I stood up and walked to the door of his office.

I told Mr. Willman that I had to get some air and walked out of the Club and into Central Park to gather my thoughts and control my anguish.

When I returned, Mr. Willman told me that the NYAC was wholly responsible for the loss of the medals and they would begin to gather other winner's medals from the four Olympics that Ray participated in and duplicate them. Once all ten had been crafted, he assured me they would be sent to me in Baltimore.

I was consumed with frustration and indecision and couldn't remember anything after the meeting other than walking across Central Park South and sitting on a park bench. I sat for a few minutes, my mind focused on that night back in 1978.

I envisioned the lobby of the Club, a dark figure slipping past the concierge and the guard who must have been sleeping on the job.

I saw the thief picking the lock on the glass doors of Ray's personal display case, silently lifting the items from the shelves, shoving them into a bag or his pockets, and leaving unnoticed.

A gust of wind scattered the letters from the folder on the bench. I scooped them up and returned to the bench. As I slipped the letters back into the folder, the one I had shown Mr. Willman, dated December 21, 1937, was on top. Since the copy of the letter my mother received in 1937 is so dog-eared and faded I will duplicate it here.

December 21, 1937

Miss Mary Elizabeth Ewry
c/o George J. Gillespie, Jr.
20 Vesey Street
New York, N.Y.

My dear Miss Ewry:

On behalf of the New York Athletic Club, I want to take this opportunity to acknowledge receipt of the athletic Trophies (medals) of your father which you have generously offered to the Club for display in our Trophy Room.

To say that we will be more than pleased to accept same under any condition which you may wish to impose. It is a distinct honor for the Club to display these Trophies. Your father exemplified everything that a true sportsman should, and we were always proud that he honored us with his association.

Sincerely yours,

ARTHUR McALEENAN

Chairman Trophy Committee

After I read the letter yet another time, I began to piece together the impact of that year on my mother. She would have been eighteen and a half years old and completely alone in the world.

My mother had been accepted to the Maryland College for Women[3] in Lutherville, Maryland in 1937 and she left home excited about what lay ahead for her.

Once notified of Ray's death after only a few weeks at school, she had to suspend her studies and return to the Douglaston, Long Island estate to arrange for the funeral.

When it came time to address all of Ray's Olympic medals and trophies, the trustees of the estate suggested she unburden herself by loaning them to the New York Athletic Club for display. Since the Club had sponsored Ray for the 1900, 1904, 1906[4] , and 1908 Olympics, she agreed.

---

[3] The original Maryland College for Women was sold in 1952 and transformed into College Manor, an assisted living facility.

[4] The Athens Games of 1906 were held as the 10th year anniversary of the 1st Athens Games. The IOC doesn't recognize the 2 gold medals, but the USOC does.

The Club's representatives assured her they would be placed securely in Ray's private display case in the grand hallway where other members' medals and trophies from Olympic competitions were on display.

After all, for many years, he was the world record holder in the standing jumping events and had won more individual Olympic gold medals than any other athlete in the world. So now the mystery of Ray's Olympic medals was born.

7

BALTIMORE – 1980

When I returned to Baltimore, I felt a deep sense of guilt. I kept blaming myself for not developing Ray's story sooner. Had I done this in early 1978, Ray's medals would be secure with the family. Feeling somewhat defeated from this setback, I dove headfirst into Betsy's archives again.

On this occasion, I opened a box that revealed some vintage pictures of her as a very young girl on Long Island in the early 1920s. Finding these pictures was not only exciting but also deeply moving, knowing that at the time I found these treasures, she was in a nursing home because she had begun to show signs of the onset of Alzheimer's disease.

She had been living on a small farm owned by her old college roommate and family while teaching at the University of South Carolina when her cognitive powers began to disintegrate.

The final straw happened one day at a traffic light. She had stopped on yellow, reached over to her pocketbook for a cigarette, and waited for the traffic light to turn green. When it did, she simply sat there, staring at the VW's dashboard. The alarming truth began to hit her, and she realized she had forgotten how to drive.

The steering wheels, the gas pedal, the gearshift…all of them were foreign to her. Shortly, horns began to beep and the impatient drivers behind her began to yell at her to get moving.

She told me later that she had panicked. Never had she felt such fear.

When a policeman came to her window, he found her banging her fists against the steering wheel and weeping from the frustration.

I found out later that this brilliant policeman was one of those southern "good old boys", and when he saw the VW Bug with Maryland tags, he deduced from her actions that this Yankee lady was drunk and delirious.

He arrested her for disturbing the peace and locked her in a holding cell.

It wasn't until the next morning, that a bright young lady thought she might have experienced a T.I.A.[5]

Later that day I received a call from my aunt, who was married to a prominent doctor at Johns Hopkins. She told me what had happened and that her husband had talked with other medical friends who suggested we bring Betsy back to Baltimore for examination and extended care, so we did exactly that.

She was relocated to a nursing home and I remember how uncomfortable I felt when I sat next to her bed. Here was the woman who had raised my sister and me to be strong and to seek happiness in our lives disappearing before our eyes.

I would visit her as often as possible, but I must say those days when the light faded from her eyes, and she stared at me not knowing who I was was gut-wrenching. I would go on talking to her as though she understood. The doctors felt she might comprehend but simply couldn't respond. I began telling her about my researching her father's life.

I sat there rambling on about what I had found in the storage unit and what an amazing man her father must have been. She had her head turned toward the window the entire time. Finally, I realized this exercise was futile. It was time to go.

When I stood and leaned over to kiss her cheek, her head turned so quickly, that I was startled. She looked directly into my eyes and I noticed her eyes were their natural bright deep blue and the light had returned. I smiled and leaned closer, kissing her soft cool cheek. As I did, I heard her whispering something to me. I didn't immediately understand what she had said, so I pulled back some.

"What'd you say, Mom?"

"Tell them…tell them he's my unsung hero."

"Ah, so you like my idea?" I asked, praying the conversation would last.

---

[5] Transient Ischemic Attack (a mini-stroke)

She said nothing, but her eyes did this weird squinting thing as if to add a sense of urgency and importance to what she had uttered.

"I will, Mom…I promise."

Her head slowly turned back toward the window and I knew the light was gone again. That moment haunts me to this day, as it was the last time she ever spoke to me. I saw her on several more occasions, but she never said a word and the light never returned.

One day late in the year, my friend Leo D'Aleo asked me to help with his newest venture; a bar restaurant located just north of Baltimore in a quaint little community called Towson. It nestles a few blocks north of what Towson State College was then.

For three or four blocks along the main thoroughfare all sorts of stores, bars, and restaurants catering to the locals and thousands of college students lined each side.

One such location was ideal for Leo and he, along with some partners, leased the property and called it "Spirits". It was refurbished in his usual classy manner with dark wood, marble bars, and a kitchen headed up by a talented chef he lured from the beach.

I was hoping to be part of the operation, but in all reality, we both knew that since there would be no live music, there wouldn't be much for me to do. After all, I was the second-worst bartender in Ocean City, Maryland back in the day.

One night, a year or so after Spirits opened, I spotted Marty Bass, a charismatic local TV personality from WJZ-TV.

I introduced myself and we sat together at the bar talking about this and that until I got about my project with Ray.

He told me he thought his sports director at the station, Randy Blair, might be very interested in speaking with me and he promised to set up a meeting. Marty could have blown me off, but a week later, keeping his promise, he called and said to come down to the station to meet Randy.

It was great to finally meet someone true to his word. Randy was a tall, handsome guy with a quiet demeanor and a mind crammed with sports knowledge. He was truly excited about Ray and my project and said that a half-hour special, or even a documentary, might be in order if he could push the idea across to the management of the station, but it might take some time. This would be my first lesson in the politics of broadcast television.

It was over a year later when Randy finally called me. After all, the 1984 Los Angeles Olympics were a little over a year away and they thought this might be a good time to begin some run-up stories to the Games.

For the meeting with Randy during Christmas week, I brought everything I had on Ray. We sat in a small room at WJZ-TV and began to do a chronological layout and script.

The last thing Randy said as we parted ways was, *"Be patient. These historical stories are tough to put across but have faith. Ray's story is not only an American story, but it's also a worldwide Olympic story and we won't let it die. We will get it out there!"*

On January 9th, 1983, Randy was playing in a charity basketball game when he suffered a severe heart attack and died on the court. I was watching TV when the report of his death came in a news flash and felt a great sense of loss. I also felt a wave of guilt wash over me as I was anguished that a man who could help me with my own goal had been taken away. It took a day or two to realize that there are bigger things in life than my selfish desires. I mourned for Randy who I had truly begun to like as more than someone who could advance my success. I miss him to this day.

A few weeks later, Marty called, and we set up a meeting.

One of the great things about Marty is his positive attitude. He said that we should continue what Randy was working on, but we might have to go about it differently.

Marty had a show called *"Coffee With"* in the six to seven a.m. time slot.

He approached his producers with the idea of having me on the show. The idea was accepted, and I again compiled some subject matter on Ray and went on TV to push my project.

Marty was great with his questions and always set me up to give long informative answers. Although Marty's *"Coffee With"* show was early in the morning after it aired I received dozens of calls from people who saw the segment.

I was booked for a few speaking engagements and had a few station affiliates call about Ray. Finally, the word was getting out and I began to realize that there were many more people who knew of Ray Ewry and his feats than I thought.

I will always link Randy Blair, WJZ-TV, and especially Marty Bass with my quest to make Ray's story known.

8

LAFAYETTE, INDIANA

In October of 1888, when Ray turned fifteen, Mary Elisha had grudgingly allowed Ben to drive Ray to school for the first time since his paralysis set in four and a half years earlier. He had become an avid student, excelling in mathematics, mechanical drawing and history.

Ray's one major failure was his ability to interact with his fellow students due to his shyness. He was very slender and almost a foot taller than most of the boys in the classes he attended and had to endure cruel remarks from the bullies and curious glances from the girls. The only girl who seemed to enjoy talking with Ray was Mrs. Johnson's daughter, Nelle, who used to bring his lessons to the house when he was bed-ridden and enduring the Polio.

It didn't help that Mary Elisha's austere lifestyle had Ray dressing in black suits, white shirts and a tie, making him look like those traveling big-tent preachers that roamed the countryside spouting salvation and trying to save the sinners. This was the reason he acquired the nickname, "DEAC"; short for deacon.

Ray's junior and senior years at Centennial were filled with hundreds of hours of absorbing his lessons, and at home, the same amount of time was spent pounding out his exercise drills.

Nothing else seemed to matter to him as he had evolved into a serious scholar and a young man whose body was transforming into that of an athlete.

His arms, shoulders, quad, and hamstring muscles had developed to the point that when he a Pup walked along the Wabash towpath Ray would occasionally stop at the side of a fence line, crouch down, and leap over it with ease.

He never tried to join in any school athletic activities at Centennial due to his fear of rejection and his self-inflicted study habits.

In March of 1890, a gentleman from Purdue University stopped by the Elisha's and after an interview with Ray told Mary Elisha that if Ray maintained his high marks through his senior year, there might be a chance that he would be awarded a scholarship for the upcoming freshman year in September.

9

BALTIMORE – 1982

After numerous calls and some uninvited visits to the New York Athletic Club, I finally received a package from them. I was thrilled to find some medals[6] the thief must have missed, or maybe just not interested in. I never knew they were part of Ray's collection.

The next day another package, five times the size of the previous one, arrived. The package contained six tarnished trophies[7] that had been presented to Ray for winning first place in various athletic events.

For the record, I would like to thank and credit the NYAC for housing and returning the remaining mementos of Ray's A.A.U. and Club medals that Betsy loaned them for display in 1937. At least they kept a portion of their part of the bargain.

---

[6] The package consisted of 7 NYAC gold medals for standing jumping events (1904 through 1908). The balance consisted of A.A.U. medals: 1 silver medal (1906) and 12 gold medals (1898 through 1910).

[7] Two of these trophies came from the 1906 Olympic Games in Athens. King George of Greece presented them to Ray personally at the awards ceremony.

In April, I felt I was running out of ideas for the project. Since I had returned the dozens of boxes of memorabilia and journals to the storage unit,

I thought I would go back and go over all the contents for the fourth time in case I missed something. I remembered there was a box in the storage unit that had some miscellaneous reference books I hadn't read yet.

I drove to the site, swiped my proxy card through the security slide, and drove toward my unit's location only to find the manager standing in the middle of the drive flagging me down.

I noticed three police cars parked near one end of the row of units and I asked the manager what was going on. She stated that there had been a break-in last night and that five units had been wiped-out. Ever the positive thinker, I felt bad for the people whose units had been burglarized and continued to my unit.

When I had parked and was walking toward my unit, I saw the garage-style door to my unit open and a policeman making notations on a legal pad. It was at that moment that I got a sinking feeling inside. My biggest fear was that I might be one of the five to have been burglarized and that fear crystallized as I investigated the empty unit. Everything was gone! I felt physical pain when I realized all of Ray's journals and diaries had been stolen.

The police informed me the thieves had parked next to the ten-foot-high, chain-link fence that separated the storage property from the I-83 North expressway, used heavy cutters to enter the compound, and sledgehammers to bash in the rear walls of the first five units they came to.

The police stated that it was probably the same team of thieves they had heard about that traveled interstate highways targeting storage compounds easily accessible from a major thoroughfare.

I had to deal with the fact that I would have to rely on recollection to portray Ray's personal accounts of his life and times and I am thankful for a good memory.

The one nagging issue that haunts me to this day is that the thieves, upon discovering their "take" and not knowing its true value, probably threw anything related to Ray into the first dumpster they came across.

In October, I had the good fortune to view Bud Greenspan's Olympic documentary "Wilma". It had an enormous effect on me. Wilma Rudolph, also a polio victim like Ray, overcame her illness and went on to become an Olympic gold medal winner in track and field.

The things I have always admired about Mr. Greenspan's documentaries were his use of archival film footage and the great staff of writers that never failed to bring tears to my eyes with their poignant narrative.

As a devout "credits" watcher, I waited for the program to finish and wrote down the name of the production company and its location. It displayed "Cappy Productions - New York City."

That was all I needed. The next morning, I called New York information again, obtained the number, and called the company. As was de rigueur for most of the companies I spoke with in New York, I was placed on hold. A minute or so later, a gentleman by the name of Sydney Thayer came on and a long-distance friendship began.

My main reason for calling had been to see if Cappy Productions had any archival film footage of the early Olympics, specifically any footage of Ray. Sydney was very open and honest, stating that he was relatively new and would do his best to search the film archives and get back to me.

I've called Sydney on many occasions through the years with the same result…no known video footage.

Sydney was a great mentor, explaining that just because there might not be any rare footage of Ray his accomplishments have been so widely documented.

Without his encouragement, I might have quit. Months went by with no contact and having been burned before, I wasn't going to hold my breath. But, to my delight, a letter from Sydney arrived in November.

The revelation that one piece of footage he had thought to be Ray was indeed Platt Adams, who took gold and silver from the 1912 Stockholm Games, was a bit disappointing.

But, his letter turned out to be a great source of contact. Two positive things about Sydney's letter were the names and contact numbers that I could call.

The first contact was a veteran freelance writer, June Becht [8], of St. Louis, Missouri. I found Mrs. Becht to be a wealth of information.

She had been researching and writing about the 1904 Olympics for many years and is considered the best person to speak with about the Games held in her hometown so many years before.

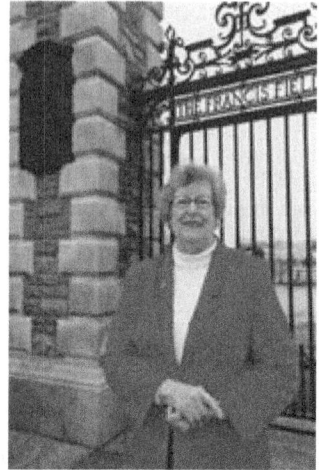

When I spoke with her, I was impressed with her enthusiasm for the 1904 Olympics. She gave me a contact name at Washington University in St. Louis and I was able to purchase some "as of yet" unseen photos of Ray.

I extend my heartfelt thanks to Mrs. Becht for her assistance with my project.

---

[8] June Becht was honored as one of the U.S. Torchbearers for the Athens 2004 Olympic Torch Relay

10

LAFAYETTE, INDIANA - 1890

Ray graduated near the top of his senior class at Centennial and as the warm spring of 1890 was turning into summer, Ray had matured into a strong, handsome young man. He had sprouted so quickly in the last year that none of the suits at the local stores would fit him.

The top red mark on the door jamb of his bedroom measured 6'4". He was slender, some said skinny, and most of his shirtsleeves were many inches too short for his long arms.

He had become adept at walking without his braces but used them when he attended a few social dances, wearing them under his trousers just to be safe. Certain popular groups still quietly ridiculed him as being that gangly kid from Lafayette. It didn't help that, when dancing with a girl, her head reached only the top button on his jacket. His clothes were too small, and he knew he looked like a country bumpkin.

Before going to the Centennial School's commencement ceremony, Mary had ordered a crisp new shirt and a tailored suit for Ray to wear. To help him with his social skills, she spent an hour the night before the event teaching him how to bend a little when dancing with a girl.

Ray's fellow graduates had never seen him in a fitted suit before and to his delight, when they saw the black suit, white stiff-collared shirt and the thin black tie, the consensus from most of those gathered for the ceremony was that he looked quite distinguished and mature and his confidence soared.

At the graduation dance, many girls who vied for a dance with him mentioned his transformation.

The next morning at breakfast she saw a new, confident young man before her. Her happiness knew no bounds as she listened to his recounting of the many girls he danced with and the change in the attitude of the boys in his class.

PART TWO

11

THE PURDUE YEARS – 1890 - 1891

In 1869, a man living in Lafayette, Indiana dipped into his immense fortune and withdrew $150,000. He presented the money as an endowment along with 100 acres of his vast Chauncey property he had purchased in 1834 for $850.00.

His donation tipped the scales in the local legislature and allowed the board of the Farmer's Institute to finalize plans for the founding and construction of a university on the property.

His name was John Purdue and because of his donations and social stature, his name was affixed to the name of the school, thus…Purdue University.

The property was located just west of Lafayette, and in 1871 leading members of the small suburban village proposed the plat to be annexed and called West Lafayette, but the Lafayette voters turned them down when they realized that expensive improvements to the aging infrastructure were sorely needed.

In 1888, across the river in Lafayette the powers that be decided due to the fast and steady growth of enrollments at Purdue, they held another vote.

The result was almost unanimous. They decided to bring the little village of Chauncey into the fold and named it West Lafayette.

For the first week of Purdue orientation and classes, Mary insisted that Ben drive Ray across the bridge to the Purdue campus. She was still very protective of Ray and concerned about his stamina.

But Ray, relishing in the joy of being unfettered from his braces, made Ben drop him off on the far side of the bridge in West Lafayette so he could walk onto the campus unassisted.

The curriculum suited Ray and he excelled from the start of his freshman year. Many of his professors enjoyed his wit and enthusiasm, especially when it came to physics and second-semester engineering studies. One item that seemed to excite Ray was the opening of the new School of Electrical Engineering.

His daily life now consisted of two things; his studies and his training which he approached with equal vigor. His study habits propelled him to be among the top five students in his class and his training was paying off with increased leg strength to the point that he even tested himself by running short distances.

Since the beginning of this project, I devoured all of Ray's personal memoirs in the *"Purdue Alumnus"* and private papers. In the end, I came up with nothing more regarding his training methods other than his descriptions in his journals.

Some days were notated only with distances, and to my surprise, there were a few days during the months that had low distances with the word "run" circled.

When cold weather set in, Ray found out he could travel to Terre Haute and join other athletes as they trained indoors at the Y.M.C.A.

Incidentally, there was no mention of any female contact other than Mabel and Mary, and no indications that he was even interested in taking time away from his studies and constant exercising.

It's obvious that Ray, possibly due to the early abandonment of his father, the tragic death of his mother when he was six years old and his life-threatening bout with polio, lacked self-confidence.

Instead of being distracted by the offers of his classmates to head out for weekend nights of what they called "a night of gaiety", Ray might have been found hunched over his draftsman's table reading about geometry, architecture, and mechanical drawing, or he might have been found lifting the heavy seed bags or leaping over the back-yard fence.

Now that he could drive the buckboard to the levee, Ray was again helping Captain Spigot unload his barge and stack the supplies in the barn. Mary celebrated young Ray's assistance, as she could keep Ben at the store all day.

She was getting older and slowing down some and having Ben there to assist was essential to keep the store stocked and ready for customers at all times.

RAYMOND CLARENCE EWRY, B. M. E.,
Assistant in Mechanical Drawing.

After an exhaustive regimen of studying and the trips to the Terre Haute Y.M.C.A. gymnasium for his training during the winter months, Ray emerged as a much-improved jumper and scholar.

As spring came to the campus during Ray's freshman year at Purdue, he began noticing the various sports venues that were in action around the campus. He began venturing out with Pup focusing on the university's track and field events.

Many students on the campus had noticed the tall, gangly freshman and when someone would inquire as to who he was, the response came simply,

"Everybody calls him 'Deac'!"

Being so much taller than most of the male students he still reminded many of the fabled character, Ichabod Crane from the Washington Irving 1820 publication, *"The Legend of Sleepy Hollow"*. Ray didn't care for the "Deac" moniker at first, but soon, he simply accepted it. It was a lot better than being called "Ichabod".

As his freshman year was ending, he had become more comfortable with his place at Purdue and his social life expanded to include many clubs and societies including the Dance Club, the Military Brigade, and the Music Club where he learned to play the banjo.

On the 22nd of May, the annual "Field Day at Purdue" was scheduled. The officers were in place and the spectators had assembled around the gravel pathway encompassing the grounds in front of the Main Building called the Oval. Most of the athletes were fully engaged in competition around the field. The dashes were beginning on the straight gravel path that began at the Main Gate.

A list of the Field Day officers was displayed on an elevated banner at the base of the steps at the Main Building.

George Ashley – Chief Marshall

N. Booth Tarkington – Clerk of Course

H.A. Huston – Referee

Professors Phillips, Stone, and Ellsworth - Judges

Professors Golden and Coulter - Starters

Mr. Goss and Mr. Lotz – Timekeepers

Ray and Pup arrived in front of the Main Building early enough to see many contestants warming up and consulting with their coaches about technique. Some were stretching on the grass inside the Oval while others were running wind sprints to loosen tight muscles in the crisp morning air.

He stated in his first Purdue journal that it gave him great encouragement to be around athletes. He admired their discipline and love of competition.

Many years later, Ray wrote fondly of his recollections in the 1919 Purdue Alumnus:

"As to the course, would the present-day athletes perform so well over the course of those days? Which same course consisted of the gravel road around the Oval running in front of the Main Building for the distance events, while the dashes were run on the cinder road leading from the main gate at State Street toward the Electrical Engineering building."

"The boys were delighted to see a long line of wheelbarrows complete with drivers positioned side by side at the start line. They were tying different class color ribbons to their frogs for identification in preparation for the Purdue Field Day Frog Race."

"Don't scoff, you modern athletes, but match this event with one calling for greater coordination of mental and muscular effort, finer judgment of pace, or more expert knowledge as to the critical number of vibrations at which frogs become restless. At least, frog racing develops restraint and character. I have yet to learn of a frog-racing addict who would so lower himself as to strike anyone, no matter what the provocation."

Ray C. Ewry - Purdue Alumnus

Ray and Pup watched the Frog Race with the other spectators and both knew what the other was thinking. It had been many years since that fateful frog race when Ray came down with his first attack of paralysis.

Any bad memories they might have had vanished as they watched the contestants scurrying along the marked course, occasionally chasing their renegade frogs to the delight of the cheering spectators.

After the Frog Race, Ray was drawn to the jumping apparatus in the corner of the grassy field inside the assigned track.

It was here that he watched a fellow classmate, Jimmy Studebaker, rack up victory after victory. Jimmy amassed seven first-place awards in the jumping and running events.

Ray stood there, mesmerized by the fluid motion Jimmy used to clear the bar for the high jump and the concentration he used to get set for the broad jump.

Ray wondered deep down if he had the mental and physical strength to compete at this level.

It was at the end of the awards ceremony for the jumping events that Ray saw Jimmy with his various ribbons, medals, and local prizes for his victories.

After the ceremony, Ray congratulated Jimmy on his successes of the day and Jimmy recommended that Ray, being so tall, might want to enter the "high-kick" event that was to take place in a few minutes and Ray accepted the recommendation.

He and Pup walked over to the pit where registered just before the cut-off. There, under the Vernon's Clothing store and Haworth's Drug store signs, he wrote his name down as an entrant in an athletic competition for the first time.

Since he was the last to sign the entry ledger, he had to stand and watch all the other competitors go before him. One after another, the lads would take a step and throw a leg high in the air. Each attempted to touch the circular metal plate dangling from the line attached to the out beam.

When it came to Ray's turn, he walked to the ground beneath the plate, looked up to gauge the distance, and took a long step backward. He bent at the waist, exhaled slowly, and with his right foot, took one long step.

His foot planted firmly and up went his left leg. His shoe hit the plate with such force that it flew up and wrapped over the out beam making it necessary for an official to climb a ladder and unwind the string for the next round.

The official at the post raised the plate three inches before the second round began.

Out of the fourteen competitors that day, only six could touch the plate, with the rest being disqualified and sent to the bench. Ray kicked the plate with relative ease during this round. The third round had the official raise the plate another three inches.

Only two men barely touched the plate and Ray easily made it three. This time the plate went up two inches.

After the first two competitors missed the mark. Ray walked to the pit, bent at the waist, exhaled slowly, and stepped off. The spectators cheered as again, Ray's foot hit the plate so hard it wound around the suspension beam again.

As the diminutive Pup ran to him and hugged him, Ray was immediately engulfed by dozens of spectators slapping him on his back and heaped congratulations on him. Pup just held onto his waist until he felt a hand on his shoulder. It was the voice of the track coach.

The coach saw Pup clinging to Ray with all his might and motioned him to let go as he wrapped an arm around Ray's shoulders and tried to walk him away from the crowd, but a group of reporters from the local newspaper clamored around them, asking the coach questions about Jimmy Studebaker and the other students who excelled during the day's events.

As the coach answered questions, Ray was presented a dozen bottles of soda water donated by Haworth's Drug store for winning the high kick. It wasn't a medal or a blue ribbon, but it was Ray's first tangible recognition of his athletic efforts.

Once the reporters had enough for their articles, the coach asked Ray to come by his office to talk about his joining the track team for the 1891-92 school year.

Ray met the coach the next morning and after agreeing to join the team, he was handed his white training tunics and shoes and told to get dressed.

Following the brief meeting, the coach walked Ray to the area of the campus designated for jumping practice.

He told him that since Jimmy Studebaker was the record holder for the high jump, he wanted Ray to focus on the broad jump.

The coach introduced him to the take-off bar and the long landing pit of the broad jump. He asked Ray to show him how he would execute the broad jump.

When Ray set his feet, the left slightly in front of the right, and crouched, the coach came over to him and pushed him down even further into his crouch, telling him to inhale deeply, then exhale and go.

Ray followed his instructions and upon his takeoff, flew almost vertically in the air. His distance was only six feet from the take-off bar. Ray was embarrassed at the short distance, but the coach told him not to worry about it.

He returned to the jumping area where the coach said he was not only the track coach but an ancient history professor as well and he went on to explain the two heavy metal objects in his hands.

That day, Ray learned about the Grecian Olympian, *Chionis*, who became the most famous broad jumper in early Olympic history with the help of Halteres.

In the 656 BC Olympics, jumpers could enhance their distances by gripping hand-carved stone weights.

They would grip these weights, get into the crouch and begin to swing their arms back and forth together. When the athlete was ready, he would swing the weights behind him one last time and leap up and out as his arms brought the weights forward. Ray noted that these stone weights reminded him of the heavy metal irons that women used to press newly washed clothing.

The next day, two hours before practice was to start, Ray brought two fifteen-foot sections of string and placed them on either side of the landing pit.

He would make five jumps with the hand weights and mark his longest jump by placing a sharpened twig next to the right side of the pit and knotting the string around it. Then he would make five jumps without the weights and mark the longest distance on the left side.

Soon, the distance between the weighted jumps and the free jumps was diminishing. He noted that after using the weights, once he abandoned them, each jump felt like he was flying. He had mastered the ability to sail up and out for ever-greater distances.

Ray finished his freshman year at Purdue ranked fifth in his class. He relished being in the mechanical drawing classes and studied deep into the night to gain his ranking.

His professors all felt that he was like "a duck taking to water" when it came to illustrating and grasping the logic of mechanical engineering.

Before he left for the summer break, two of his professors suggested various books to read. He devoured them in the first two weeks of the break and even wrote a short thesis on steam hydraulics to be handed in when school started up again.

Throughout the summer months, Ray would do his drills in the barn and the backyard and wait for Pup to show up, so they could run on the towpath.

He loved the freedom of being able to run, but it took a toll on his body. He found that his hips became sore and his lower back muscles cramped after a strenuous run. It bothered him somewhat because he wanted to be able to enter both standing and running events in the coming track season.

BALTIMORE - 1983

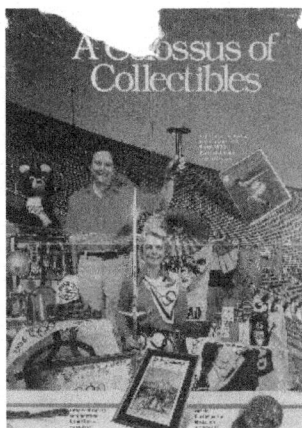
A Colossus of
Collectibles

I came across an article in an issue of "*LIFE*" magazine about a California couple named Torney who was one of the premier Olympic memorabilia collectors in the United States.

After I read the article, I went back to the cover page to view the many items placed as "overlays" by the magazine's art department and was immediately drawn to the "playing card" on the page. It was a card with the image of Ray in his pre-jump position for the standing high jump.

Blindly over-confident in my abilities to track down anyone even remotely related to my project, I got on the phone and called San Diego information searching for the Torneys.

As lady luck was still smiling at me, I was given their number and called them. Mr. Torney couldn't have been more surprised and seemed excited to speak with me.

We had a great conversation about Ray and my small collection of memorabilia. He gave me a brief history of how he and his wife had traveled the world attending many Olympics and adding to their ever-growing cache of Olympic collectibles. The sad ending to the call was the revelation that he too had been through a painful theft of many of his items that were stored in a block-like storage unit very similar to mine.

The thieves entered the same way they did in my circumstance by smashing through the rear wall of the unit with sledgehammers. I extended my condolences while telling him about my theft and we both commiserated about how targeted we both felt.

I ended the call by telling him how happy and proud I was to see my grandfather's image on a card on the page.

I thought a lot about the similarities of our thefts and came to a final opinion. I firmly believe to this day that the break-in of Betsy's storage unit and the loss of Ray's memorabilia were coincidental, whereas the Torney break-in was planned and executed by thieves who had gone to great lengths to locate the exact unit and steal the valuable Olympic mementos.

After I hung up, I looked at the Torney page again and something triggered a recent memory, so I went to my archives and rummaged through the many smaller items I had compiled, and low and behold...I had that exact same card. It came from the Mecca Cigarettes "Champion Athletes" series from the early 1900s.

13

PURDUE – 1891 - 1892

Ray's sophomore year at Purdue found him embracing the new curriculum. He approached his art and history classes with the same enthusiasm as he had with his mechanical drawing and electrical engineering classes in his freshman year.

He had brought his incredible ability to focus on the athletic field too, and there is no better example of this trait than the Indiana Intercollegiate Games in Terre Haute.

The train ride from Lafayette to Terre Haute was a very uncomfortable trip for the Purdue track team. In his journal, Ray recounted that no more than an hour out of Lafayette a terrible rainstorm enveloped them. He described the shafts of lightning and the thunder that kept the team on edge for most of the trip.

They arrived a bit fatigued but anxious to compete. He noted that the level of confidence was sky-high, and the team was eager to take the field to prove to the other colleges that Purdue was a school to be reckoned with.

It was a glorious day with the event fields surrounded by the various college and university supporters cheering for their school's athletes. The Purdue athletes did their best to compete with the other schools, but no one could defeat Arnold Layman from Rose Polytechnic.

Layman had championed the 100-meter dash, the running high jump, standing high jump, and pole vault in the 1890 I.I.A.A. games.

He went on to lead Rose Polytechnic to the I.I.T&F championships in 1890, 1891, and 1892. He established new state records in the high jump and 100-meter dash.

All that Layman's competitors could do was to stand by and watch him out-distance everyone from every school. Ray, ever the student, was quite impressed and he studied the flawless techniques of this amazing athlete as much as possible.

Ray knew the mechanics of any jump were simple in theory, but he began to realize that there had to be a combination of perfectly executed elements within the jump for it to be successful.

It was quite a challenge to whip those long legs of his far out in front of his body and reach for his shoes as if doing toe touches. He wished he had worked more on the landings instead of the takeoffs.

When it came time for the standing broad jump competition, Ray was somewhat surprised at the attention his coaching staff bestowed upon him. It was as though he was the star of the team, and it embarrassed him.

There were five entrants for the standing broad jump, each getting three jumps in the rotation. After the take-off official dropped his flag to start the first rotation, three jumpers fell backward and touched the sand with their hands, thus greatly lowering their distances. Ray was fourth in the order and performed a respectable jump, but not as far as the last athlete.

A roar exploded around the landing pit as the hometown boy from Terre Haute came in first. The noise and excitement of the event had attracted the attention of Arnold Layman.

He stood taller than most of the spectators and Ray noticed him off to the side as he approached the foot bar for his second jump.

Ray went into his drill...standing tall with his arms above his head and breathing in and out.

In one smooth move, he simultaneously dropped to the crouch as he swung his arms behind him and then threw his arms forward and up as he pressed his shoes onto the jump bar, exploding skyward down the pit. He landed a foot and a half farther than the longest jump of the rotation so far. The crowd applauded as they saw the measurement. The hometown athlete tried but failed to make Ray's mark on his second attempt. So now the stage was set.

Knowing they couldn't compete, three competitors bowed out for the third and final rotation.

The track official said that there would be a coin flip to see the order of the two remaining jumpers. With the coin coming up tails, Ray was told by the referee he would be jumping last, so Ray moved closer to the pit to watch the jumper from Rose-Pullman.

The young man seemed nervous, but once he stood on the foot bar he seemed confident. The official dropped the small start flag and he went into his crouch and exploded down the pit, landing two inches beyond Ray's last jump. The partisan crowd erupted. The jumper was engulfed with his supporters, praising him for a grand effort. They all seemed to have already given him first place.

While the broad jumps were going through the rotations, more events had begun near the landing pit. The discus and pole vault events had attracted large noisy crowds.

As Ray approached for his final jump, bursts of cheers would assault the small entourage of broad jump spectators who were hushed for the final jump. The competitors for the 100-meter dash were setting up at the start line as Ray stepped onto the bar. His arms stretched over his head, he began the in and out breathing and went down to the crouch for the lift-off.

Just as he reached the bottom of the crouch and was about to lift off, the starter pistol for the dash went off. Ray, startled by the loud blast, felt propelled up and out with more thrust than normal.

Later, he explained he felt as if he was jumping in slow motion. He said he saw the heads of the spectators on both sides sliding past him as he soared through the air. He remembered how hard his knees hit his chest as he extended his body out over the pit.

He landed perfectly, and his momentum carried him into a forward tumble. When the feeling of slow motion left him, the roar of the spectators alerted him that something very special had taken place. This was Ray's first championship and he knew this was what he wanted from that moment on.

During the long silence that followed, Ray remembered thinking of the years of pain, the evolution of his training drills, and especially of Kate.

He was somewhat saddened that he couldn't remember exactly what she looked like anymore, or even remember what it felt like to drop into the peach basket for the daily leg exercises that were such a major part of his early regimen as a young boy.

In the early days of August, Ray and Pup constructed a simple high jump in the barn. Into two support beams ten feet apart, they hammered heavy nails into the beams in measured, six-inch increments. Pup sought out and found a straight tree limb and placed it on the lowest nails and the custom high-jump apparatus was complete.

Pup used a pitchfork to loosen the dirt on one side of the limb, so the landing would be softer than the hard-packed floor.

Once they were satisfied with the high jump, Pup used a three-foot section of railroad tie he found in the back of the barn. He buried it almost flush to the ground and dug up a long, narrow patch of dirt floor for the broad jump landing pit. Now Ray was free to practice his jumps no matter rain or shine.

Once the colder weather halted all outdoor events except football, Ray was content to focus on his classes and afterward, found time in the early evenings to practice in the barn, but soon it became too cold even for that.

On May 18, 1892, Ray watched his new friend and mentor, Jimmy Studebaker, as he broke the state record for the standing high jump by leaping over the bar at the height of 4 feet-7 inches; an inch over the old record. He also won the high-kick and the tennis doubles championship.

Just before Ray's jump, Jimmy came over to the landing pit. To Ray's surprise, Jimmy said he was withdrawing from the standing broad jump competition due to exhaustion and bade him good luck in the contest.

Later, Jimmy told friends he knew he couldn't beat Ray and that he felt Ray would become the greatest jumper ever. The track coach had somehow worked the official and had Ray jumping last. Ray watched the third round go quickly and so far, the longest jump of the day was 9 feet-4 inches. Ray stood focusing on the jump and his technique.

He began to swing his arms out and back. On the third arm swing, he dropped down to a crouch, coiled his body, and exploded up and out over the landing pit.

Again, his mind went into slow motion…his eyes on the end of the pit. He landed hard on his heels and rolled to his left as the spectators roared their approval.

One official stuck the start of the measuring tape next to the edge of the take-off bar as a second official walked backward letting out the tape and placing it next to the impression of Ray's heels in the mixed sand and sawdust.

When the distance was written on the elevated chalkboard, Ray was lifted onto the shoulders of his cheering teammates and paraded around the pit to the delight of the Purdue spectators.

After breaking the Indiana state record of 9 feet 10 inches by half an inch, Ray became somewhat of a celebrity.

His abilities were not only recognized on the athletic fields but in the classroom as well. One day, while doodling in his mechanical drawing class, he was asked to join the team of illustrators for various publications on campus. His forte was the intricate free-hand filigree called for on the illustrated lead pages of many campus publications.

In the summer of 1892, the Purdue varsity football team's coach approached Ray. He had seen Ray training for the track team next to the football practice field and was impressed with his athletic abilities.

He felt that Ray might make a good end. Ray was very skeptical of his ability to run like the other football players and declined, but he let the coach know that he would include running as part of his training regimen.

14

PURDUE - 1892 -1893

Around the time the new semester began, news of a new sport created in the previous year by a Canadian, Mr. James Naismith, spread west to Indiana. Naismith was at the forefront of coaches who recognized the need to promote good conditioning while athletes waited out the long winters indoors. His solution was to create a new indoor sport called basketball.

He attached a peach basket to a flat board and elevated the basket to a height of 10 feet. Once a player had successfully lobbed the ball into the basket, an attendant stationed near the basket would quickly climb a ladder and retrieve the ball. Praise should go out to the individual who thought to simply cut out the bottom of the basket.

Naismith had begun to train coaches at the International YMCA in Springfield, Massachusetts and once they had learned the 13 fundamental rules of the game, he came up with the idea of dispersing these trained coaches to teach the game. They fanned out across the country to introduce the game to Eastern and Mid-Western colleges, several universities, and selected YMCA locations, stressing the value of continued conditioning.

By the time Ray's junior year began, he knew the paralysis he endured as a child was behind him. The soreness and stiffness in his joints after his training sessions or a long, arduous competition were looked upon as part of the process of recovery. He had asked local trainers and coaches many questions about how to maintain flexibility and came to the realization that he had to train constantly.

So, when inclement weather blew into Lafayette, Ray traveled to the YMCA gym to play this new sport.

When the weather permitted the track team to begin practicing outdoors, Ray had reached a point in his development where he was constantly bettering his distances in the standing high jump, standing broad jump, and the hitch kick.

On one day in April, he was standing near the broad jump landing pit when Jimmy Studebaker approached and told him he was leaving Purdue and taking a position with a firm in Chicago. Ray was sad to see his friend and mentor leave but was bolstered by Jimmy's kind words of encouragement.

It was the last time Ray ever saw Jimmy, but he thought about him often for the rest of his life. He made a special note in his journals that Jimmy Studebaker was the one person who influenced him the most in his early years of competition.

Due to a mild winter season, Ray could practice late in the year before the cold weather set in. This added time allowed him to perfect his take-off and landing techniques so that each jump was a lesson in discipline. Knowing Jimmy Studebaker would not be competing this season, Ray felt obligated to carry on the winning tradition at Purdue.

May 19, 1893, was not what trackmen would consider ideal weather for a meet. It had rained the night before and the morning offered up a light fog. It was the day Purdue had scheduled its annual Field Day competition.

The sun broke through the clouds and burned off the early morning ground fog by nine a.m., but the field grass was still wet and the landing pits for the various jumps were sodden and mud-like.

That afternoon, Ray was invincible. He attacked each event with quiet confidence. In the "one-foot-on-ground" event, he reached the height of 7.0 feet, winning first place. In the 2-step hitch-kick, he touched the plate at 9.0 feet, winning another first.

In the jumping events, Ray watched all his competitors do their best and then went on to dominate the standing high jump, winning first with a jump of 5.1 & ½ feet.

After a short break, he exploded off the jump bar for the standing broad jump and landed 10.5 & ½ feet down the pit for the top place win.

For his final achievement, he even won first place in the running high jump with the bar set at 5.6 and ½ feet. Unfortunately, Ray had never landed in a muddy pit before.

When he landed on the other side of the high bar, his feet slipped out from beneath him and he felt a painful twinge in his knees. He said nothing but knew he was injured.

As someone as aware of their body as Ray was, he knew he would have to rest and recover from the awkward landing and the effect it had on his knees.

15

PURDUE - 1893 - 1894

After the Field Day mishap in May, Ray's competitive season was over. He suspended all training to recover from his knee injuries. Each night after dinner he wrapped his legs with hot towels and mentioned to Mary, as an afterthought, that doing this reminded him of the old days of his paralysis treatments.

After a month of no training, Ray felt his thigh muscles getting loose and he knew he had to start building up his leg strength to where it was in May. Since the rawhide strip that went behind his neck caused him discomfort, he began using an old broomstick placed across his shoulders to hold the heavy seed bags hooked in notches at each end.

He had started with lighter weights but shortly was squatting with the bags that totaled over 100 pounds. By late August his thigh muscles had grown stronger than before his injury.

He knew he was ready for the new track season when one day in early September, he went to the practice field on campus and raised the bar to five feet. It was close to dusk and no one was on the field.

With no crowd noise and no one to distract him, he stood next to the bar, went into his crouch, swung his arms back and forth as he was trained, and vaulted off the grass, clearing the bar by an inch.

As he stood in the landing pit looking back at the bar, he smiled with confidence. Satisfied with his effort, Ray sat quietly on a bench near the landing pit and thought about how he could improve his style.

But his was not the only smile. There were two others.

One was on the face of his track coach who had watched him from his office window in one of the administration buildings. The other smile beamed from the face of Nelle Johnson who had been walking with some of her girlfriends along the path that bordered the campus athletic fields.

As the group moved on, Nelle told them to go ahead as she wanted to talk to Ray about something.

Satisfied with his jump, Ray sat down on a bench near the path. He saw Nelle standing by a tree and waved. She was about to approach him but pulled up when the coach sat down next to him and handed Ray the local campus newspaper from Princeton.

This was the day that two events happened to Ray that would influence the rest of his life. The first was his introduction to Baron de Coubertin by way of a newspaper article. The Frenchman was in the country trying to gather support for a new concept for something called the Olympic Congress and the possibility of setting up an international athletic competition.

The coach's friend, Professor William Sloane of Princeton, was meeting with the Baron to discuss expanding the scope of an International Olympic Committee being constructed with the sole purpose of creating an international series of events.

The second was the realization that Nelle Johnson, the girl who in his lonely, bedridden years had brought him his lesson plans and books, had blossomed into a strikingly beautiful young lady. Ray wrote that this was the moment he began to care about what others saw in him...and what he saw in others...especially the fairer sex.

It wasn't until the start of his senior year at Purdue that Ray resumed his training. His knees had taken a long time to heal, but by sitting on the flatbed of the buckboard and attaching a heavy seed bag to each foot, he would extend his leg straight out to build the knee and quad muscles back up to their former condition.

At Purdue, he devoured every book he could find on engineering and mechanical drawing and tested so well, that he moved up to third in his class and maintained his high-grade average throughout the first semester. He continued to impress his professors with his ability to absorb their teachings.

As the track season began in the spring of 1894, one of his academic advisors approached him and asked what his plans were after graduation.

He admitted he hadn't thought much about it but was open to ideas. The advisor intimated that during a meeting of the staff, his name, along with two other students, was brought up in matters regarding the possibility of hiring them to be student teachers.

It meant that if Ray wanted to continue his studies for his Master Of Engineering Degree, he would be considered for an Associate Professor position in the Engineering Department at Purdue. He would be paid a modest stipend that would help with expenses and be able to complete his studies for his Master's Degree.

Ray didn't accept the idea of continued studies immediately, stating that he had to confer with his family before making his decision.

Once Ray told Mary about the offer and saw her excitement at the prospect of him obtaining his M.E. degree, he accepted the offer. This one decision allowed him to chart his academic and athletic career for the next four years.

He was now free to focus on furthering his education in engineering without worrying about finding a profession, and it would allow him to be a major player on the Purdue track & field team for more inter-collegiate sporting events.

At the Field Day events in the spring of 1894, Ray continued to amaze people with his jumping abilities. Word had spread through the midwest college athletic community that there was a jumper from Purdue who was breaking records right and left.

On this day, representatives from seven schools had come to see the Purdue Field Day events and one athlete in particular. Ray did not disappoint them. He broke three Indiana state records in the standing high jump, standing broad jump, and even in the hitch kick event.

His teammate and best friend, Robbie Robertson, was a star on the Purdue football team and after seeing Ray's strong showing in winning the running high jump, he urged him to try out for the football team in the fall. Ray was confident in his running ability due to his training along the Wabash for the last two years and told Robbie he would consider the offer.

On the morning of his graduation, as he dressed for the ceremony, Ray heard Mary talking to someone downstairs. He had been given his robes and mortarboard the day before and was looking in the mirror noting how short the robe was when he recognized Nelle's voice.

When he came downstairs, he greeted the ladies and found that Nelle had asked Mary for a ride to the ceremony because her father's carriage had a broken axle.

Later, at the commencement ceremonies, as Ray was handed his diploma by the university president, Nelle leaned over to Mary and commented on how proud she must be. Mary smiled when she looked at Nelle and saw nothing but admiration and affection in the young girl's eyes.

16

PURDUE - 1894 - 1895

For the first post-graduate semester of the year, Ray was assigned to assist professors John J. Flather and Richard Smart in classes focused on hydraulic pumps and special machine design.

One day, in a casual meeting, Professor Smart told Ray he had an uncanny ability for machine design and suggested he enroll in classes taught by another professor who had a reputation for being one of America's best resources for advanced industrial design.

The professor introduced Ray to a new and different concept in engineering. What if the engineer took raw materials and created something with them? Then, he would discover what it would be like to see something he had made, not just conceived and put down on paper.

The professor's name was Laura Fry[9], and before coming to Purdue, she had invented a technique of applying pigment evenly to ceramics by using an atomizer which she patented while a member of the famous Rookwood Pottery Company staff.

Being the daughter of Henry Fry, a famous woodcarver in Cincinnati, she had also learned woodcarving at an early age and even surpassed her father's reputation for the craft.

After coming up against creative differences, she left Rookwood and was hired by the Lonhuda Pottery Company.

Unfortunately, she soon found that Rookwood was using her special technique without her permission or sharing profits from her inventive methods. She also discovered that many of her completed pieces had been removed from public display.

She had information that the carvings had been taken by senior administrators of Rookwood for display in their own homes.

[9] Barbara Streisand and Steven Spielberg are avid collectors of rare, early Laura Fry pottery and woodcarvings.

Once Ray enrolled in her class she quickly recognized his talent for wood carving and design. She worked closely with Ray and the results of his winter inactivity proved to be quite rewarding.

The hutch, silver cabinet, and hinged jewel box pictured here were designed and hand-carved by Ray between 1900 and 1908.

PURDUE – 1895 - 1896

When the track season began in the spring of '95, Ray was unanimously elected captain of the team. The motto, "lead by example", had been planted in Ray's mind many years before and he led the team's effort at the Field Day events by dominating all his jumping events. He posted the following distances during the events.

Standing Broad Jump: 10.6 & ½ feet

Standing High Jump: 5.2 feet

Standing High Kick: 9.2 feet

Running High Jump: 5.6 & ½ feet

In August, Robbie Robertson was happy to see that Ray had taken him up on his suggestion that he try out for the 1895 Purdue football team. Ray told him he felt very confident that his running abilities were now sufficient to get him on the team.

D.M. Balliett, the Purdue coach, had relocated from an east coast university, so his style of play was different than the "run-run-run" game plan the Big Ten schools applied in their offensive scheme. Coach Balliett was a friend of the coach from the University of North Carolina at Chapel Hill and had been told of the forward pass, although illegal at that time, and how some referees would toss a coin to dictate whether a touchdown resulted from a forward pass would be counted.

The UNC coach used the forward pass in a game against the University of Georgia, but the attending official disallowed the score.

He wrote the Purdue coach that he should take a chance at throwing the forward pass and maybe if it results in a touchdown, the official might allow the coin toss.

On Ray's first day of football practice, he sat through the indoctrination meeting between Coach Balliett and the new members of the team where he learned the first team to play for Purdue was formed in 1887 and the colors, "Old Gold and Black", were chosen by the team's captain that year. Ray wrote in the journal about his college years that he got a big kick out of the origin of the name "Boilermakers".

It seems in 1889 the coaches, seeing the volunteers who showed up for the team's first practice were rather small and didn't seem cut out for such a physical sport, recruited some rather husky Monon railroad boilermakers and even some tough policemen. After they were enrolled in just one class to make them legal students, the team went on to win game after game.

After the drubbing of the Crawfordsville team, the local newspaper called the visiting Purdue team Boilermakers, Haymakers and Sluggers. Shortly after the publication, Purdue students who read the very uncomplimentary article about the players on the football team voted to use "Boilermakers" as the team's official name.

Ray made the team and secured a position as a second-string end. Coach Balliett was excited to have a tall end and secretly worked with the quarterback, A. P. Jamison, on plays involving the forward pass to Ray as a trick play.

On October 29th, the University of Minnesota came to the Purdue campus for a very physical confrontation. To add to the excitement of the game, Ray's childhood nemesis, Pully Ironshire, was on the defensive team for the visitors.

The local Lafayette paper hailed the game as Pully's homecoming and touted a real battle would take place. Ray knew how Pully was and warned his teammates to be aware that the big man was prone to "bending the rules". He didn't know how profound the statement was.

In the fourth quarter, with the Minnesota team ahead by 18 points, Coach Balliett threw caution to the wind and called for the forward pass to Ray. Pully had enjoyed blocking Ray all afternoon since his bulk was most often too much for Ray to push around.

As the team broke the huddle for a designed play, Ray went to the opposite side of the field and set himself up in a crouch, ready to shoot down the field.

Pully began screaming about a trick play and raced behind his defensive line to cover Ray. As the play started, Ray exploded down the field, chased by Pully. Ray was a step ahead of Pully as the ball was thrown and as he turned to look for the ball, Pully grabbed his jersey, slowing Ray down enough for him to leap on his back.

It seemed to the spectators that Ray was carrying Pully on his shoulders for a few yards as the ball arched its way toward them. As one of the biggest men on the field, Pully used his 230 plus pounds to slam Ray to the ground.

His left shoulder hit first, and Ray felt the muscles tear as the ball sailed over the two men who had crashed to the ground. Ray, thinking his shoulder was dislocated, was assisted off the field to an accompaniment of "boos and whistles" from the Purdue faithful.

At the end of the game, Purdue had been outscored 24 to 6 and the coach was reprimanded for trying that kind of forward pass trick play and never to call it again.

Ray wrote that he knew his football playing days were over, but he was more concerned that the injury to his shoulder would inhibit his flawless take-off technique when the track season began in the spring. It was the last football game Ray ever played.

SIGMA NU FRATERNITY – BETA ZETA CHAPTER

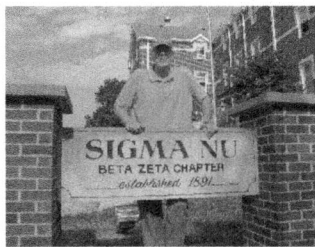

In June 2013, the Grand Historian of the national Sigma Nu fraternity, Mr. Robert McCully (San Diego State), visited Baltimore, Maryland for a quiet breakfast and an interview about Ray before moving on to the national headquarters in Lexington, Virginia.

When asked about my knowledge of Sigma Nu, I had to admit that the only experience I had with the fraternity was thanks to former Indiana State Representative Joe Micon who, during a visit to the Purdue campus, took me to the fraternity house.

We had the pleasure of meeting a bright young man named Luke, the president of the Beta Zeta chapter of Sigma Nu at that time, and shown the plaque depicting Ray's 1982 induction to the Sigma Nu Hall of Fame.

Thanks again go to Mr. McCully for telling me that along with Ray Ewry, both Zane Grey, the author of many popular western novels, and Glenn Miller, the famous bandleader from the 1930s and '40s had also been inducted into the fraternity's Hall of Fame.

Mr. McCully has written a fine article about Ray in the national magazine for Sigma Nu, the *Delta*, and I'd like to thank him for spreading the word about "UNSUNG" to all the fraternal brothers across the country.

Also, thanks to Mr. McCully, I discovered Ray was inducted into the Sigma Nu fraternity on September 26th, 1896, so…it stands to reason Ray pledged during the spring of that year.

I can only imagine this was quite a week for Ray.

Not only did he join the brothers of Sigma Nu, but just before the track season started, Ray was again elected to be captain of the track team and on May 29, 1896, when Ray was in top form for his events.

At the Indiana Intercollegiate Championship against Rose Polytechnic, he equaled or broke the state record for the standing broad and triple jumps and broke the world's record with an astounding 5.3 feet & ½ inch effort in the standing high jump event. This was the first time Purdue had come in first place at any Indiana Intercollegiate meet.

After the events, no less than three representatives of different athletic clubs approached Ray. One organization, the Chicago Athletic Association (C.A.A.), seemed like a good idea for Ray to consider after his days as a collegiate athlete and his duties as an associate professor had ended.

When the men from the C.A.A. produced a newspaper that recorded the victories in April at the 1896 Summer Olympics in Athens by members of their organization, Ray was quite impressed.

19

PURDUE – 1896 - 1897

In his final year as a post-graduate student, he spent many months traveling around Indiana examining various adaptations of the car lighting systems in train cars. It was an important subject because many railroad companies' reputations had suffered greatly due to fires caused by faulty ventilation and the imperfect design of the lighting systems in passenger cars.

Ray had designed a carburetion system for the gaslights that greatly diminished the chance of fire by regulating the mixture of air and gas. Ray wrote his thesis entitled, *"Test Results of Carburetors of Railway Car Lighting"*.

As a Student Assistant in Mechanical Drawing, his credentials allowed him to meet and converse with all levels of railroad employees. These men always received him as an approachable academic who cared about their industry, and one who was dedicated to the safety of their mode of transportation with an eye to the future.

The track team had lost some talented athletes to graduation the year before, and on May 12, 1897, at the final Intercollegiate Meet in Chicago, the Purdue men finished in third place. Earlham came in first by one point over Rose Polytechnic. Although disappointed, his teammates could hold their heads high thanks to Ray's individual performances. Ray's winning measurements were recorded as follows:

Standing High Jump – 5.3 feet & ½ inch

Standing High Kick – 9.2 feet

Standing Broad Jump – 11.0 feet (World Record)

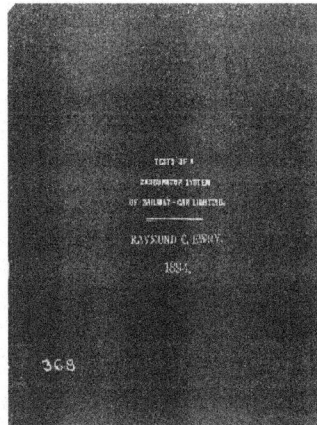

On the day of the graduation ceremony, Ray was presented with his master's degree in Electrical Engineering and elevated to the role of Assistant Professor of Machine Design and Kinematics, and was given a position on the staff.

Although he was tempted, he knew he didn't want to be cloistered as a university professor for the rest of his life and respectfully declined. His thoughts were of international athletic competition and finding a well-paying job where the real sports action was.

He enjoyed his years as an associate professor, but he wanted to apply his knowledge and ingenuity in a "hands-on" environment. While speaking with athletes from the east coast, he realized New York City was where he wanted to be there.

In August 1897, Ray had been invited by officials of the seven-year-old Chicago Athletic Association to come to Chicago for an interview. Ray knew his days of intercollegiate competition were ending and he wanted to continue his career in field athletics.

He traveled north and accepted the offer to wear the "Cherry Circle" emblem and represent the C.A.A. in the rapidly growing arena of amateur club competition, primarily against the New York and Boston Athletic Clubs.

20

BALTIMORE – 1983

In March, I moved into a quaint "Williamsburg" style brick gatehouse situated at the entrance of a long, tree-lined driveway on the estate of the Marburg family. The family had a piece of the horse named *"Deputed Testimony"* that later won the 1983 Preakness.

A few weeks after settling in, I received a phone call from Bill Mallon, one of the two people Sydney Thayer of Cappy Productions had recommended I contact. Bill told me he would be passing through Baltimore on his way back to medical school at Duke University and asked if I had time to meet with him. He was welcomed with open arms as Bill seemed very interested in Ray, his trophies, and the A.A.U. and NYAC medals.

I was impressed with Bill's story of his years as an amateur golfer and how he was twice voted to the list of "Outstanding College Athletes of America" and went on to join the PGA from 1975 through 1979.

As a medical student, Bill was interested in Ray's history and amazed that he had defeated Polio by applying nerve-jarring exercises for his therapy. We also spoke deep into the wee hours of the morning about the theft of Ray's medals. Finally, I set him up with an air mattress in the living room and retired.

I woke early and made Bill what I hoped to be acceptable coffee and breakfast. Before he left, I asked him one final question about writing the Ray Ewry story and he simply said, as Jim McKay and many of the pundits had said.

"You can't simply write about Ray's Olympic experiences. You have to let the readers know of his battle with Polio and how he reconstructed his life through athletics."

Bill went on to write about sports injuries and in 1987 launched his career as an orthopedic surgeon.

He added a second career as the medical editor for *Golf Digest Magazine*.

His fascination for the Olympics produced over twenty books on the Games and he is considered one of the leading Olympic authorities in the world. He is also co-founder of the *International Society of Olympic Historians.*

The organizing committees of both the Atlanta and Sydney Olympics valued Bill so much he was hired as their historical consultant for the Games.

The International Olympic Committee *(IOC)* contracted Bill as a consultant statistician and to his credit, he was awarded the *"Olympic Order"* in 2001 for his specialized services to the Olympic movement.

I lost touch with Bill for many years until my newfound enthusiasm for the Ewry project blossomed again. When I read his biography during my internet search, I was amazed at what he had accomplished since that night in Lutherville.

I will always be indebted to Dr. Bill Mallon for pointing me in the right direction and for his encouragement to never give up the quest to enlighten the world about Ray's story.[10]

---

[10] There is a comprehensive reference to Dr. Mallon's books on the Olympics at the end of the book.

21

LONG ISLAND - The Travers Island Games - 1899

William Travers, the famous Wall Street tycoon, had purchased the property on Long Island Sound in 1886 and created a summer home for athletes from the New York Athletic Club. There were over thirty acres of various athletic fields and training facilities.

The focal point of the property was the Main House, a grand three-story mansion that looked down at an Olympic-sized saltwater swimming pool complete with lounging cabanas for event spectators.

During the planning stages, Mr. Travers gave directions to build venues set up for tennis, lacrosse, rugby, soccer and even a champion-caliber croquet course. Just off the Island, rowing and yacht races could be observed from the shoreline.

Ray, representing the Chicago Athletic Association, came to Travers Island and marveled at the venue. He was entered in two events; the standing high and standing broad jumps. Ray wrote that on this trip to New York, he was humbled by the caliber of the athletes that attended these Games and noticed that most of the athletes from the east coast seemed to take the facility for granted, while athletes from mid-western schools and clubs were very impressed with this modern sports venue.

He tried to keep a low profile but standing head and shoulders above most of the athletes made it impossible. He accepted the stares from many who had never seen such a tall, gangly athlete enter the jumping events. But they soon found out that "Deac" had come to compete….and to win.

As was his custom, he quietly went about his disciplined routine, defeating the current record holders in both events.

Once he finished his final jump, Ray was approached by a representative of the prestigious New York Athletic Club.

He spoke to Ray about various lucrative career options working for the United States Navy at the Crescent shipyards in Elizabeth, New Jersey and if Ray approved, he would set up a meeting.

Ray was surprised that the man had full knowledge of his successes in academics at Purdue and thought his Master's Degree in Engineering would go far in obtaining the open position as Assistant to the Inspector of Machinery. He also said that he was sanctioned to offer Ray a position on the NYAC track team if he moved to New York or New Jersey.

On the long train ride back to Lafayette, Ray's head was filled with thoughts of working for the U.S. Navy and competing for the NYAC, but he was somewhat concerned about his relationship with Nelle and what she might say about his desire to move to New York and begin a new chapter in his life.

He had thought of her often during his trip to Travers Island and as the train approached Lafayette, butterflies churned in his stomach as he fingered the little blue velvet box in his coat pocket and plotted how he would ask her a very important question.

LAFAYETTE - SPRING - 1899

The news of the offer from the U.S. Navy was a double-edged sword for Mary Elisha. At first, she allowed her protective tendencies to dictate the conversation, but when Ray explained that he yearned to expand his horizons by moving to New Jersey and working for the U.S. government, she realized Lafayette couldn't hold him.

She was thrilled to hear about the offer from the NYAC and believed he was destined for greatness on the national stage of competitive athletics. But, when he finally told her of his plans to ask Nelle to marry him, she broke down and cried as she looked into the little blue velvet box from a New York jeweler. Her tears were joyous since she had felt for years that Nelle would be the perfect girl to be the foundation of Ray's happiness.

Nelle had been visiting her father in Illinois for a few days and upon her return, Ray invited her to a famous Purdue campus landmark, "The Rock" where Ray kneeled, offered the ring to her, and asked for her hand in marriage.

Nelle was silent for some time. Seeing his disappointment, she told Ray that she did love him and that yes, she would marry him, but since he was thinking of moving to New Jersey and his success there was questionable, she wasn't sure the timing was right.

He realized she was correct to think ahead and knew he would have to get settled and prove that their new life away from Lafayette would be comfortable and held the promise of long-term security.

A week after Ray left for New Jersey, Nelle received her first letter.

Dearest Nelle,

Greetings from New Jersey! The train ride from Lafayette was pleasant, due to the amenities of the Pullman and the wonderful restaurant car. The food was surprisingly delicious, and the trip east was uneventful save for some raucous college athletes heading to an event in Philadelphia.

I am feeling very homesick for you, my family, and my quaint little hometown. Everything here moves so fast. I have assumed the position of Assistant to the Inspector of Machinery and Installation for the U.S. government at the Crescent shipyards here in Elizabeth.

There is quite a bit of secrecy surrounding the shipyard as we are developing vessels for the United States Navy. Every morning there is a meeting regarding the status of our Navy around the world.

Due to the volatile nature of conditions around Europe, Asia, and South Africa, there is talk of the shipyard getting more government contracts for specific types of ocean-going vessels in case of possible U.S. involvement in conflicts in the future. I am censured from disclosing anything more because of national security restrictions.

I had to rush around to find a place to stay and finally found a suitable three-room place four blocks from the shipyard.

It is so very strange not to be able to walk out my front door and amble over to the campus and put in a few hours of training.

I miss the trees, the canal, and all my wonderful friends, but you are the one I miss the most. I have embraced the hard reality that this is where I should be to move forward with my career and our lives.

The New York Athletic Club contacted me and extended an invitation to come into the city and tour the Central Park South location. I believe they will offer me a slot on the track and field team.

I'm very excited to think I might be a member of one of the most exclusive athletic clubs in the country, as most of the best athletes in this area are members.

If I am accepted, I'll be competing in the Aegean Club Games as a member of the NYAC for the first time, and hope I represent them well.

I visited the city yesterday and as I walked the noisy streets, I thought about how much you would love the milling crowds and the noise of the city itself. You could not imagine the number of people here. I have never been in a city with so many people…literally, thousands walking the streets every day. There are many buildings higher than anything we have in Lafayette, so tall that they literally block out the sun.

My dearest Nelle, it is truly exciting and I hope to be able to whisk you away from our beloved flatlands of Indiana and bring you to the thriving heart of America. I hope you are taking good care of the velvet box. Maybe you should open it occasionally and think about our future. I also hope your studies are going well and your last year at Purdue will be instructive and fun for you.

Please forward my best regards to your mother and father and if you happen to see Mary Elisha, Mabel, or even Pup, please say hello for me and extend my best wishes for their health and happiness.

It's time to retire as I have a very busy schedule tomorrow, so I send my deepest affections to you. Please know I think of you every day and more every night.

As soon as I have a chance, I will return to Lafayette. Write when you can and stay as lovely as I remember you to be.

Your boy,
Raymond

23

NEW JERSEY – 1899

Dear Rayme,

It was wonderful receiving your post. So much has been happening for me here. I am finally a senior and loving it. I have been involved with many activities and social clubs but will be happy when I graduate.

The sad news is that Captain Spigot was found lifeless on his barge that ran aground a mile north of the levee. I'm not privy to the cause of death, but it is said that he died with a jug of liquor in his lap and a contented smile on his face.

Mrs. Elisha told me that there was a short will in his desk wherein he left his two mules to her. She was very pleased, as Ben is getting on in years, and keeping the grounds proper has become somewhat of a chore for him.

Mother and father approached me about your velvet box last week when they visited the campus. They were in my room when mother happened to see it on my nightstand and opened it. I told them of your proposal and they seemed tentative but happy that their darling daughter had such a fine man asking for her hand.

I had to be open and honest and tell them what I told you. I can think only of getting through the last year of my education before entertaining thoughts of marriage. They agreed with my decision and they asked me to send their best wishes for your new career.

Lately, I've been involved with a group of students who are counseling young orphans from Lafayette. I find it very rewarding to be able to guide these lost children in a direction that might improve their lives in the future. Be well and think of me lovingly and know I am saving the next dance for my favorite Rubberman.

With great affection and kisses,

Nelle

INTRODUCTION TO PART THREE

Before I begin Part Three, I think it best to alert readers that the events that occurred during the early Olympics held between 1896 and 1908 have been written about by some of the greatest sports researchers in the 20th and 21st centuries.

For that reason, I have not attempted to cover the vast, redundant information about all the courageous athletes from these early games, but focused on those athletes and coaches who met or influenced Ray Ewry as he set out to conquer the world of standing jumping events, both at the university level in the 1890s, the athletic club competitions in the early 1900s and the Olympic Games from 1900 through 1908.

I might be criticized for not covering Baron de Coubertin and the organizers of these early Games, along with the talented athletes from the U.S. Olympic Teams in-depth, but if I did, this biography would be ten times as long. The omission of lengthy background material regarding legendary sportsmen is by no means meant to be disrespectful. I feel better writers than myself have combed the world's archival photos, manuscripts and long-lost memoirs to bring forth their wonderful stories of patriotism and their desire to lead men onto the world stage of sport.

I would like to mention the two men who had a major influence on Ray Ewry's years of competition. The first was A. G. Spaulding, the founder of one of the world's largest sporting goods companies.

The second was James. E. Sullivan, an early member of the Amateur Athletic Union and "czar" of the American Olympic Committee, and Director of the 1904 St. Louis Olympics.

In the beginning, and throughout the book, my focus has been to present to readers Ray Ewry's inspirational journey along with my struggles to unearth information about his many accomplishments, both on and off the athletic fields.

My thanks go out to the early newspaper columnists from the New York Times and the many writers from around the globe for their contributions through the years to my research. I am humbled by your talent and dedication to telling the story of the Olympics and hope that I might add this body of work to the vast array of books on the Olympic Games.

PART THREE - THE OLYMPIC YEARS - 1900 – 1908

24

NEW YORK CITY – 1900

On June 16, the NYAC held the 64th Annual Travers Island Games. The weather was cool and although menacing rain clouds hovered over the vast splendor of the Long Island athletic complex, it never rained. The Pelham Manor clubhouse was brightly decorated with bunting and banners. Dozens of yachts were gaily trimmed with flags and pennants of all colors while moored in the adjoining creek.

The throng of spectators, numbering between six and seven thousand strong, had come to see some of the best track and field athletes on the east coast. The one letdown for them was the announcement that the University of Pennsylvania hurdles and broad jumping star, Alvin Kraenzlein, would not be competing, but the level of enthusiasm remained high.

No national or world records were broken that day, but the overall performances of the athletes thrilled the spectators and as the day ended Captain Charles H. Sherrill stood on the massive front porch of the Clubhouse and petitioned the audience for quiet as he announced the members of the NYAC who had been chosen to travel to Paris and represent the Club at the Paris Olympic Games next month.

The names he mentioned, M.W. Long and Dixon Boardman (both quarter milers), John Flanagan and Richard Sheldon (both weight-throwers), Bascom Johnson (pole vaulter), and Ray Ewry (standing high, broad and triple jumps), brought loud and enthusiastic applause from the crowd assembled on the grass.

Ray was standing to the side of the audience and was completely surprised by the decision.

He noted in his first journal of the new century, that he was consumed with what he called "butterflies" in his belly and his heart began to race with anticipation.

Before leaving for Paris, Ray declined two event invitations so he could rest up and put his personal affairs in order before the trip. He had telegraphed Nelle and Mary Elisha of his good fortune and received best wishes for success from both. Nelle's Western Union telegram was terse, but it almost lifted Ray off the ground.

"Wonderful news (stop) All Purdue behind you (stop) Mother-Father approve (stop) Ring on finger (stop) Missing you (stop) Love, Nelle"

He had been waiting to see those words since the day he moved to New Jersey. If it weren't for the fact that he was about to represent his Club team and the United States in international competition, he would have hopped on a westbound train immediately.

The six Club members selected to compete from the NYAC in the Paris Games were afforded 24-hour access to the gym and lodging while at the downtown Central Park South location. Ray was granted an abbreviated work schedule at the shipyard as the management was thrilled to have such a highly-recognized star athlete in their midst.

On the morning of their departure, the American athletes assembled at the pier for final instructions while the throng of relatives and friends gave them a colorful send-off as the athletes climbed aboard the huge steamship *"Patricia"* to begin the nine-day ocean voyage across the Atlantic.

PARIS, FRANCE – 1900

When the *"Patricia"* docked in Le Havre, the athletes were somewhat surprised to find only a few dozen American ex-patriots were there to greet them as they were used to being welcomed as celebrated athletes by their American supporters wherever they went.

When they inquired as to the low-key image of what they thought would be a highly regarded and well-received sporting event featuring the best athletes in the world, they were told that the emphasis in Paris was on the "L'Exposition Universelle Internationale de Paris," which had opened on April 15th.

When they arrived at the start of the Paris Games, they were disappointed that many foreigners were there for the Exposition, and most had no idea there was to be a world-class athletic spectacle. There was no mention of the "Olympics" anywhere. Most of the press covering the events simply called the athletic event "the Paris Championships".

Ray wrote Nelle that he was happy his lodgings were only five blocks from the Pre-Catalan on the Bois de Boulogne where the track and field events were to take place. The Bois was located along the western edge of the *"16th l'arrondisment"*[11] near the suburb of Boulogne-Billancourt.

He was also thrilled to be able to wander about Paris studying and drawing many historical buildings and structures since his events were days away.

---

[11] Refers to a district in the city.

He was very impressed with the recently completed Eiffel Tower and the massive globe erected near the tower's base and on the day, he and some of his teammates reached the top of the Tower, he noted that the panoramic view of Paris afforded him the best view of the magnificent architecture of the ancient city.

The only time Ray portrayed any anger in his writings was the description of the theft of his Eastman Kodak camera by a young Parisian street thief who had waited near the observation railing at the top of the Tower for a decent grab.

When Meyer Prinstein had become somewhat dizzy from the height, Ray had placed his drawing pad, pencil, and camera on the decking and moved to bolster his friend. That was when the young thief grabbed the camera and fled down the stairs. Ray tried to catch him, but the youth was so quick on his descent, that Ray gave up and returned to aid his friend.

He noted in his 1900 Paris Olympic journal:

"The first evidence of French hospitality was the theft of my beloved camera. As I stood at the top of the stairs of the Eiffel Tower, I watched the young scoundrel, wearing a red beret, scamper down the stairs. I thought to give chase but realized my twenty-seven-year-old legs would be no match for the damnable thief."

In July, a week before the jumping events were scheduled to commence, Ray suggested to his NYAC mates that they put in some training, as he was beginning to feel like a mere tourist and wanted to maintain his focus and peak physical condition.

The group left the hotel and met some of the athletes from the Boston Athletic Club with the same idea, so they walked along the Route de la Grande Cascade to the designated area in the *Bois de Boulogne* called the *"Jardin Du Pre-Catalan"* and found that there was no cinder track as was the custom for almost all colleges and universities in America.

He was greatly puzzled by the fact that there was no high jump, no landing pits, or anything that resembled a track venue. The men rationalized that the officials simply hadn't prepared the grounds yet, as it was a week away from their contests. They decided to train anyway by jogging laps around the large, uneven grassy field.

Later that week, Ray and two companions were invited to visit the Exposition by some proud American ex-patriots. Ray, ever a student of electrical engineering, was excited to visit the Gallery of Machines.

It was inside the main room that he met Monsieur d'Avigne, a Cambridge graduate who spoke perfect English, and over a glass of red wine and croissants, gave his opinion on the abysmal way he felt the athletic events were located around Paris. He spoke of the great expectations of many French athletes for the Paris Games to represent the glory of sport and not just the French Revolution.

Monsieur d'Avigne, himself an avid sports enthusiast, had retired from competitive cycling and told Ray he was appalled when he learned that the athletes in the swimming events had to compete in the swift-moving currents and filth of the Seine.

When Ray asked him about the track and field events at the *Bois de Boulogne,* he laughed out loud and said they would be lucky to get some French prostitutes to hold broomsticks to jump over.

In his first letter to Nelle, he wrote of his apprehension.

My dearest Nelle,

To be here in Paris without the one I love is most painful. I have imagined us walking along the various avenues and through the magnificent gardens of this ancient city. It is truly a city for lovers.

I had the chance to visit the Exposition and I must say it rivals, if not bests, the one in Chicago. I was drawn to the Gallery of Machines and spent nearly the entire afternoon with a Frenchman who gave us a tour.

The new inventions displayed at the Exposition are rather amazing. I have seen an actual moving sidewalk, complete with vertical poles for which to hang on to as it slides next to the street. I also saw talking movies, a giant telescope, and a diesel engine running on peanut oil. That was quite impressive, but I don't think my mates at the shipyard would condone its use for our vessels. Someday, I must bring you to this beautiful city.

Monsieur d'Avigne, my tour guide, opined about the lack of concern the city officials have for the international competition. It seems that Mr. de Coubertin's ideals have been cast aside and the entire scheme of athletic events has been pushed deep into the shadows of the Exposition. They are more interested in making money from the admissions and the hundreds of costly vendors.

The other overshadowing event coming up is Bastille Day. The national holiday will draw out almost the entire city's inhabitants with more political than sports-minded mentalities. I shall not alarm you with petty grievances my lovely, but I feel I must portray what the conditions are regarding my events.

I happened to visit the Bois de Boulogne and found it void of any athletic apparatus whatsoever. The runners who accompanied me were dismayed at the revelation that there was no cinder track and they would be competing in all events on the uneven landscape.

I will be greatly surprised if one or more don't injure themselves, what with the many humps and dips in the ground that they must cover.

We begin the track and field events on Saturday, July 14 and I shall write with the results immediately. I so looked forward to being here, but now all I think of is you and our marriage. My feelings for you far outshine the City of Lights and I wait impatiently to return to you.

With the greatest love,
Your Raymond

26

THE RACING CLUB OF FRANCE – Saturday, July 14

Due to nerves or simple anticipation, Ray had awakened before the sun on this opening day of the track and field events, aptly titled in the program and admission tickets for the day, "Championnats Internationaux".

When he arrived at the site of the events, the sun was just coming up over the trees that lined the grounds. He found a crew of French laborers lining the various sprint and dash lanes with lye as he walked across the early morning, dew-covered grass.

A gendarme stopped him and asked in broken English to see his ticket and identification. Ray produced the proper papers and was about to walk away when he turned and asked the sleepy gendarme if he knew where the jumping events were located.

The gendarme shook his head and with palms up and extended out from his sides in the French mannerism that implied, "I don't understand", he pointed toward the other end of the large grassy park and gave the gesture again. Ray saw a thin length of twig on the ground, picked it up, held it up laterally with one hand, and simulated going over the twig from one side to the other.

"Ahh," said the gendarme. "Le Sauté en Hauteur" (high jump) and pointed to the left side of the field. Ray shook his hand and as he headed toward the designated area for his jumps, he heard the gendarme call out, "Bon chance, Mon Ami!"

Ray had learned enough French to respond, "Merci, Mon Ami!"

Ray finally found the high jump apparatus by scanning the grounds until he saw two square vertical poles.   They had been planted in the ground with a crossbar attached to each pole. The crossbar was resting on two square sliding boxes. A stretch of rope went up the side of each vertical pole, through an eye ring at the top, and then down again to a cleat at the base of each pole that allowed officials to raise or lower the bar.

As he approached the apparatus, he noticed another athlete in his French competition tunic stepping on the grass on one side of the bar. The athlete introduced himself as Emile Torcheboeuf. It took less than five minutes for Ray and Emile to become very comfortable with their attempts at understanding each other.

With little difficulty, it became clear to Ray that this pleasant man was entered in some of the same events as he and they both commented on the sogginess of the grass on both sides of the bar.

At the end of their conversation, Ray said, "Bon chance", and was surprised when Emile placed his hands-on Ray's shoulders and gave him the customary "two cheek buff kiss" used in Europe when meeting or saying farewell to someone.

After dinner on Friday, Ray retired to his room and found a thin booklet had been pushed under his door. The International Olympic Committee (IOC) had designed specifications and rules by which each event was to be performed. These rules were written in the language of every competing country and given to each team leader for all international teams to read and agree upon before the Games began.

The rules for Ray's events read:

"The feet of the competitor may be placed in any position but shall leave the ground only once in an attempt to jump. A competitor may rock forward and backward lifting heels and toes alternately from the ground but may not lift either foot clear from the ground or slide it along the ground in any direction."

When Ray received his booklet he immediately disagreed with the description of the pre-jump ethic. He found through his training, that it was very dangerous to rock back and forth on his heels and toes on the lift-off bar for the broad jump.

It makes the chances of losing one's balance so much greater, and if the jumper falls off, it is considered a failed attempt. He preferred to remain flat-footed until the moment just before lift-off to include the calf muscles as well as the quads into play when exploding up and out.

When the sun rose into the clear blue Parisian sky above the Pre-Catalan, it became evident the weather would be ideal for open field competition. Little by little, athletes, coaches, and officials filtered onto the grounds, excited to get the most popular events of the Games underway.

As the running heats began, Ray was disappointed at the low turnout of spectators. He was informed by Emile that all of France was celebrating Bastille Day, their day of revolution. Ray knew from his history classes that this holiday was the French equivalent to the 4th of July in America.

Large tents had been erected overnight to protect the food vendors who were commissioned to feed the athletes and staff.

As Ray and his teammates sat among athletes from other countries, they overheard many an outcry aimed at the organizing committee regarding scheduling and the deplorable conditions for an international venue.

"The bloody hurdles are made from 30-foot splintered telephone poles crossing the track!" cried one Englishman.

The two quarter-milers, Long and Boardman, were highly upset that there was no cinder track.

They had walked the marked-off course and were amazed that the officials expected the runners to race across the uneven grass of the Pre.

The issue that upset the American team the most had to do with the French officials and the organizing committee's scheduling of events on Sunday, July 15th. Many of the men were devout Christians or represented church-affiliated schools and refused to compete on the "Lord's Day".

Early in the morning, an American representative went to the Event Committee and presented a formal written complaint signed by the members of the American team who refused to compete on the 15th of July.

The Committee held an impromptu vote and declared that they would move all the events back to Saturday the 14th, even though it was Bastille Day, and doing so would lengthen their time at the Bois de Boulogne.

The Americans returned to the team and gave them the good news. The athletes were told to wait for their events to be announced. The officials had scheduled the qualifying events for the discus on Saturday and the finals on Sunday.

Richard Sheldon was the favorite, but there was a very serious problem with the landing area for the discus. The French had set it up in a lane between two rows of very thick trees. The competing athletes would have to make an almost perfect throw between the trees to get a score. Unfortunately, most of the attempts hit the trees and were discounted.

During the finals on Sunday afternoon, the Hungarian champion, Rezso Bauer, placed first with a toss of 36.04 meters (118.3 feet), the Bohemian star, Frantisek Janda-Suk finished second with a throw of 35.14 meters (115.3 feet), and Sheldon, with only one clean throw, came in third with a 34.60-meter (113 & ½ feet) toss.

Sheldon and the rest of the discus throwers were upset at the ludicrous conditions they had to put up with. Even the top three winners complained vocally and signed the written petition of complaint to the French officials, but as most of the letters of the complaint did, they were ignored.

Meyer Prinstein and Alvin Kraenzlein had competed against each other on the college circuit for years and this was the weekend that one of the most heated rivalries in Olympic history came to a boil.

Kraenzlein was credited and praised for his new "bent-leg" technique for the hurdles.

He had abandoned the old-fashioned method of jumping over the hurdles with both feet tucked under the body. Instead, he found great success by lifting a lead leg straight out in front of his body just as he approached a hurdle and bent the trailing leg backward and out to the side. He perfected the technique and as evident by his record of winning results, was unbeatable for years.

In 1898, as a Syracuse University student, Prinstein was entered in the New York Athletic Club Games and won first place in the running long (broad) jump, breaking the world's record with a leap of 7.24 meters (23 feet 8.875 inches).

In 1899, Kraenzlein, a University of Pennsylvania graduate, out-distanced Prinstein at the IC4A Championships, pushing him to second place with a jump of 24 feet 3.5 inches.

In 1900, before the Paris Games, Prinstein again beat Kraenzlein by leaping a world record distance of 7.51 meters (24 feet 7.25 inches).

On that Saturday, on the grass at the Bois, Prinstein easily beat Kraenzlein in the running long jump. He did so even though he was Jewish, and this day was his Sabbath. After the event, both men met to make a pact, a gentleman's agreement if you will, not to compete on Sunday, the 15th. The French Olympic officials had approved a jump-off between the two on Monday.

True to his word, Prinstein stayed away from the Bois that Sunday, but Kraenzlein had spoken to some officials and had found that some of the events they had promised to move to Saturday were indeed to be held on Sunday.

Kraenzlein broke his word and competed in the running long jump. After six attempts, Kraenzlein bettered Prinstein's mark by 1 centimeter, giving him first place and Prinstein second.

On Monday, the 16th, Ray came to the Bois early and met Emile at the high jump area near the border fence where Emile withdrew a folded piece of paper and handed it to Ray.

Ray couldn't translate all the words but saw his name and a depiction of his scissor-kick style for the standing high jump and was humbled that the French would print something like this, especially before his jumps.

He thanked Emile and wished him good luck in his attempts.

SAUT EN HAUTEUR DE PIED FERME

Le sujet qui a exécuté ce saut est l'Américain Ewry.

Comme ses autres compatriotes, M. Ewry emploie une méthode spéciale; il présente le flanc à l'obstacle, se projette en haut et un peu de côté, puis, dès que les ischions sont arrivés un peu au-dessus de la corde tendue, il élève une jambe et lui fait franchir l'obstacle en la tenant fortement fléchie, le genou contre la poitrine. Dès que cette jambe a franchi l'obstacle, il élève l'autre, qui le franchit à son tour de la même façon, pendant que la première s'abaisse et reçoit le poids du corps sur le sol.

Fig. 15 — Épure d'un saut en hauteur, de pied ferme, par l'Américain Ewry.
(Se lit de gauche à droite. On a éliminé deux images sur trois sur la pellicule chronophotographique, afin de faire sentir dans la figure les principales phases du saut complet.)

La série des mouvements se lit très facilement dans l'épure de ce saut (fig. 15). Pour éviter la confusion, les images au lieu d'être superposées ont été légèrement déplacées d'une quantité constante.

Anticipation for the jumping competition was high. It was customary for each athlete to perform three jumps and the best of the three would be his distance for the final qualification.

The weather had warmed, and some competitors were complaining of having to wait long periods in the heat and humidity between their three attempts.

As the standing high jumps were announced, Ray moved away from the athletes milling around the bar and went into a crouch.

He thought back to the day Jimmy Studebaker had shared a simple technique to concentrate back at Purdue and he needed to apply it today. He stuck fingers in his ears to silence any distractions as he went through a visual of the jump in his mind. Many athletes watched him during this ritual and shook their heads at this strange display.

Most of the early jumpers had difficulty with their take-offs, but two American jumpers, Lewis Sheldon and a native American, Irving K. Baxter from the University of Pennsylvania, had cleared 4 feet 11 inches and 5 feet respectively. When Ray came out of his pre-jump ritual, he vigorously congratulated both men on their attempts.

Content that he was ready, Ray walked toward the take-off area next to the high bar for his first jump. Suddenly, he heard a commotion over in the group of American athletes under the tent.

He tried to blank the angry voices coming from the group, but his focus was shattered when he saw Prinstein and Kraenzlein face-to-face screaming at each other. Prinstein had found that Kraenzlein had lied to him and ignored the pact they had made on Saturday.

He was livid and demanded they have a jump-off on Monday to make the competition fair. Kraenzlein scoffed at that suggestion and turned to walk away.

Suddenly, Prinstein hauled off and hit Kraenzlein in the face, knocking him backward into the circle of athletes. Charles Sherrill and a few men on the American team broke up the altercation.

For the second time that morning, Ray crouched and inserted fingers in his ears. A minute later, he stood, walked to the grassy take-off area next to the high bar, and stood sideways in silence.

A small, curious crowd was standing behind the temporary retaining fence eagerly awaiting the jump. As the official standing a few feet from the bar raised the "quiet flag", Ray took a few deep breaths, went down into his trademark crouch with his arms swinging back and forth, and exploded skyward.

After he completed the scissor kick and felt his feet land in the soft dirt, he knew he had made a clean jump.

RAY FWRY

The kinvful youth who grew up to win ten Olympic championships, winning the standing high jump at Paris, 1900. Note the opacity of spectators.

The American team, as well as the spectators, erupted in loud cheers as the realization hit them that Ray had just cleared the high bar at the height of 5 feet 5 inches. He had won his first international jumping event.

Since all three standing jumping events were scheduled on this day, Ray had little time to relish his first victory.

He waited impatiently as Mike Murphy, the trainer, rubbed his calves and thighs in preparation for the next event...the standing long jump.

After an hour, he heard the announcement for the athletes to come to the long jump area. Ray left the American tent and walked there with his teammates, Robert Garret and Irving Baxter. He was adjusting his NYAC tunic when a touch to his arm caused him to turn. He saw his new friend Emile standing there with a grim look on his face.

Emile was feeling depressed that there were so many elite athletes competing against him. Ray had a short, encouraging conversation with him and wished him well.

It must have done Emile some good because he performed a very respectable long jump of 3.03 meters (9 feet 11 ¾ inches) from the bar. The partisan spectators behind the fence cheered and waved the French flags they had been given at the admissions gate earlier.

It was now Irving Baxter's turn on the take-off bar. Wearing the University of Pennsylvania "P" on his tunic, he began to move up and down, bending his knees and moving closer each time to a full crouch.

He finally went down all the way and lifted and out in the standard technique for the long jump, landing 3.135 meters (10 feet 3 ¼ inches) down the length of the pit. Again, the Americans roared their approval for his flawless jump.

As Ray's turn at the bar came and he approached the take-off bar, Emile stood off to the side pointing to Ray and telling a Parisian newspaper reporter, *"Il est comme une homme grenouille!"* ("He is a human frog!") This nickname stuck with Ray throughout his time in Europe.

Ray smiled politely and gave a slight hand wave to Emile as he stepped onto the bar. Again, never wavering from his disciplined routine, Ray went into the crouch with his arms swinging back and forth, exhaled one last time, and blasted up and out over the pit.

His eyes focused on the tops of the trees bordering the Bois as his arms and upper body shot up and out over the pit. At the last second, he pulled his knees up to his chest and extended his legs.

His shoes landed with such force dirt sprayed more than six feet outside the landing pit. His forward momentum had carried him beyond the pit and he laid in the warm grass, sucking air into his lungs. He felt this was a clean jump and so did the rest of the spectators.

They exploded into applause and shouts as the 3.30 meters (10 feet 10 inches) distance was written on the elevated slate board. Ray had won his second Olympic gold medal.

A few hours later, in the heat of the afternoon, the trainer, Mike Murphy, was rubbing down Ray's legs when he noticed swelling in his knees. As Murphy wrote a notation in his training journal, he mentioned his concern, but Ray simply brushed him off. Of all the standing jumps, the triple jump[12] is technically the hardest to do.

---

[12] This jump was also referred to as the Hop, Step and Jump or the Standing Triple Jump.

It requires the athlete to stand with both feet on the bar, take off (or hop) from the bar with both feet, split his legs in mid-air, and land on one foot.

Next, he must push off with the landed foot and land on the other foot completing the long step portion, and then he must push off with the second landed foot and tuck into the familiar bent position for the long jump, landing with both feet in the pit.

Seven members of the American team, Ray Ewry, Irving Baxter, Robert Garrett, Lewis Sheldon, Frank Jarvis, John McLean and Daniel Horton walked quietly side by side to the jump site with their arms resting on the next man's shoulders like an advancing phalanx from the Roman army

A small group of athletes from other countries watched with envy and some intimidation. Emile and the reporter from Le Monde stood and marveled at the wall of athletes approaching them.

When the seven Americans began belting out college chants as they walked to the jumping venue, the porter said, *"Ces Américains sont sauvages!"* ("These Americans are savages!")

27

PARIS, FRANCE - Bois de Boulogne

Per their best-recorded jumps in their national competitions, each athlete was placed in a graduated "lowest to highest" order. The shortest distance would be the first jumper and so on until the jumper with the longest recorded distance would be last.

The jumpers from Hungary, Sweden, and Germany were first through third and then the Americans were set with Ray being last due to his longer distances in earlier competitions. Because of the large number of competitors, the jumps took quite a long time.

Each man made his first and second jump, and at the end of round two, the standings were Garrett in third place, Baxter in second, and Ray Ewry in first.

Round three had attracted hundreds of spectators. Many shielded themselves from the sun with umbrellas while reporters wrote frantically on notepads while numerous international athletes began to make bets on the outcome of the standing triple jump.

Once the jumping resumed, the American athletes drifted apart, and each gave their best effort. Robert Garrett logged his final distance for third place with a leap of 9.50 meters (31.2 feet).

Then, Irving Baxter thrilled the spectators with a huge jump of 9.95 meters (32.7 & ¾ feet). As he brushed off the dirt from the landing pit, he shook his head disconsolately, knowing it would not be enough to beat the tall man from Indiana.

Baxter was correct.

Ray approached the take-off bar confidently, planted his feet, went into the now-famous crouch with those gangly arms swinging back and forth, and finally launched off the bar.

In his Olympic journal, Ray admitted he had made the mistake of using the long (broad) jump technique of bringing both legs up in a tuck under his bent upper body.

In mid-jump, he realized his mistake and tried to lower his right leg, but it was too late for a solid landing.

He landed on the heel of his right foot, spraying dirt from the impact. His momentum caused him to lurch forward in an awkward motion, but somehow, he adjusted and managed to push off with such power that he landed a little left of center in the pit.

He knew he was in trouble after the second portion of the triple jump, so when his left foot landed, he blasted up and slightly to the right, tucking his knees under his torso and aiming for the trees to complete the final stage of the jump.

He landed roughly and rolled forward, slamming into the last few feet of the pit and out onto the grass. He laid there, his lungs fighting for oxygen in the heat of the day, and noticed the only thing he heard was his breathing and his pounding heart. Slowly, he heard what started as a gentle hum build to a crescendo of deafening noise. His teammates screaming wildly, they rushed over and piled on top of him.

He had won his third consecutive jump with a distance of 10.58 meters (34 feet 8 & ½ inches). This day proved to be an amazing display of focus and determination to win. Ray had done the unthinkable, winning three gold medals in one day.

At the age of 26, when most athletes had retired from competition, he had accomplished something none other had even thought possible.

At the awards ceremony, the president of the French Olympic Organizing Committee (FOOC), Viscount Charles de la Rouchefoucauld, presented Ray with three sterling silver trophies for his record-breaking jumps.

The original photograph which has been published in almost every book and reference journal focusing on the early Olympics displays some of the members of the United States team.

The group is comprised mostly of members from the NYAC posed just before the 1900 Paris Olympics at the Bois de Boulogne.

Back row: *John Tewksbury, Bray, George Orton, Alvin Kraenzlein, Grant, I. K. Baxter,*

Middle row: *Frank Jarvis, Josiah McCracken, Johnston, Ray Ewry, Charles H. Sherrill, (manager, NYAC) Robert Garrett, R. Sheldon, John Flanagan, Mike Murphy (trainer)*

Front row: *Boardman, Newton, Maxwell Long*

The United States Olympic team had the good fortune to be coached by Mike Murphy who was called the "Father of American Track Athletes" for the United States Olympic Teams for the 1900, 1908, and 1912 Games. His coaching years were spent mostly at Yale from 1887 through 1913, but he also split his time coaching the NYAC athletes at the Travers Island compound from 1890 through 1901.

Once the track and field events had taken place, the athletes stayed on in Paris for another week to become spectators themselves and to cheer on their fellow countrymen.

Kraenzlein and Prinstein refused to speak to each other and had to be kept separated when the entire team was taken "en masse" to various celebratory events in their honor.

It became clear that Ray was a phenomenon and the French press lauded his feats. They had many nicknames for him.

The most popular ones were, *"La Grenouille Humaine"* (The Human Frog) and *"L'Homme de Caoutchouc"* (The Rubber Man). The other team members got quite a kick from the French press by being nicknamed, *"Les Sauvages"* (The Savages).

In the end, the Paris Olympics proved to be somewhat of an embarrassment for the French. They had kept Baron de Coubertin, a man praised and respected for his organizational skills and ability to work with international committees, away from the Games. This proved to be a major *"faux pas"* on their part.

The French newspapers also exposed the mishandling of the Paris Games through numerous on-site interviews with athletes who told of the scheduling mishaps that caused many of them to miss their events. The track and field venue at the beautiful Bois de Boulogne was labeled outrageously inadequate and might as well have been held on a farm.

But, to Ray and most of the athletes on the American Team, the journey to Paris and the final team results were very satisfying.

My darling girl,

As luck would have it, your boy did quite well in Paris. Due to the high temperatures during the scheduled jumping events, my muscles were loose and felt fluid and strong. I took first in all three events and I must congratulate the other competitors for their spirited efforts.

We should be arriving in New York in a few days and once there, I will telegraph you. I am thinking more and more that the time is right for us to become husband and wife. I can only hope your mother and father are ready for a son-in-law. The one thing that has bothered me is my inability to formally ask your father's permission for your hand in marriage in person.

A friend has informed me of a very nice two-bedroom home to let and I am going to see it once I get back. I am proud of you and wish I could have been in Lafayette to see your graduation. I am sure your parents were just as proud and excited for you.

Be well, my dearest Nelle and know I love you and think of you always.

Always your boy,

Raymond

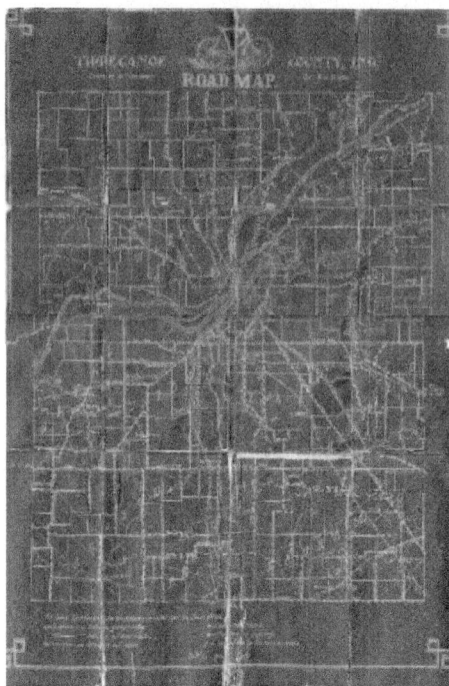

BALTIMORE – The Tippecanoe Bike Map - 1986

As far back as I can remember, I had always had this "blueprint" style map of Tippecanoe County, Indiana hanging on my bedroom wall. When I asked my mother what it was, she explained that it was a bicycle map Ray had drawn of the county to be published for local cycling enthusiasts while in college.

Once I moved into a new apartment, I hammered a nail into a bedroom wall and was about to mount the frame, when it slipped from my hands, shattering the glass and destroying the wooden frame. I gently withdrew the map from the frame and broken glass. It was very brittle and could crack and fall apart if handled roughly.

I placed it out on my bed to smooth out the many folds and as I ran my hand across the surface, I felt a lump under the map and carefully turned it over.

I discovered Ray had created this map to be protected by folding it into a 4 by 6-inch shape and taping a hand-drawn cover on both sides. I was thrilled to find he had taped three photographs of Ray and Nelle I had never seen to the back of the cover.

Ray had written about his new camera in his journals and judging from the photos I suspected the timeline might be in the late 1890s when Ray was an associate professor of engineering and Nelle was a student.

NEW YORK CITY - 1900

As they began to disembark, the American athletes were greeted as national heroes by thousands of people at the dock. The Mayor of New York City, accompanied by a brass band, was also there to greet them.

Ray was happy to be back home and when he finally arrived at his front door, he found four letters from Nelle and a stack of newspapers delivered while he was in Paris. He eagerly read all of Nelle's letters and was overjoyed to find that she had selected three alternative dates for the wedding in Rossville, Illinois. Ray immediately went to the telegraph office nearby and composed a quick telegram to Nelle giving the go-ahead for two of the three days.

When he returned to work, he was welcomed by the commander of the shipyard and taken to a large construction hanger where he found all the employees, from upper management on down to the labor force, waiting to honor him for his performances in Paris. The management had set up a vast food table and gave all the workers the rest of the day off.

Before Ray left the shipyard that day, he had a brief meeting with his immediate superior and told him of his plans to be married in Illinois and was granted a two-week leave of absence.

The wedding took place in Rossville, Illinois on October 17, 1900. Although Nelle and her mother wanted formal invitations, there wasn't enough time, so they printed simple scripted announcements to be mailed to family members and close friends.

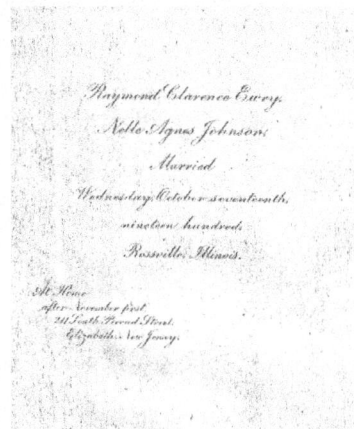

Many university friends attended the ceremony as well as relatives on both sides. Mary and Mabel took the train from Lafayette and brought many gifts from the well-wishers who could not attend.

There were many tears shed when Nelle's family realized their daughter was leaving for the east coast and it might be quite some time before they saw her again.

When they returned from the wedding, Ray and Nelle settled into married life. Nelle went about furnishing the apartment and became involved in charity work in the community, focusing on the plight of poorer families and orphaned girls. Ray began work on a secret engineering project for the Department of the Navy related to a new type of vessel aptly described as a "torpedo boat".

To stay in peak condition, Ray trained at the Travers Island Club when weather permitted and the downtown NYAC when inclement weather forced him inside.

Nelle adapted to life in New Jersey but gently hinted to Ray that the many hours he spent at the shipyard and training at the NYAC caused her to feel somewhat lonely. Ray decided to decline many requests for jumping exhibitions and focused on making his new bride happy by adjusting his schedule so he could be with her for longer periods.

In May of 1901, Ray signed up for the popular Knickerbocker Games and went head to head with a formidable triple jumper, Dr. Mulligan[13], who had equaled Ray's record in the standing triple jump. Ray's 34.8-foot jump broke the world's record.

Later that year, he represented the NYAC at the World Championships in Buffalo, New York in September, winning the standing triple jump.

Ray also established a new world record in the standing high jump by clearing the bar set at 5.5 feet & ¼ inches.

---

[13] I have found no record of Dr. Mulligan's first name.

In 1903 during the Faitlin Games at Celtic Park, Ray broke the world's record for the standing triple jump again. After this record was made, Ray was considered the most formidable standing jumper in the world.

In January 1904, Ray and Nelle had settled happily in their new home in Bayonne, New Jersey, but before the end of the month a single telegram from Mabel Ewry Hunt, Ray's newly married sister, brought the contented atmosphere at the Ewry household to a halt.

Mary Elisha, the woman who had raised Mabel and him since they were orphaned 25 years earlier, was gone and Ray was devastated. The Ewry's were on the first train out of New York City, headed back to Lafayette. The article in the *Lafayette Journal & Courier* on January 28th stated: *"She fell on last Sunday and fractured her right hip, an accident which was responsible for her death."*

The funeral was held on Saturday when mourners paid their respects to Ray and Mabel. Ray wrote about his displeasure toward the end of the wake when many men spoke to Ray about his efforts in Paris four years earlier and expressed their hopes that Ray would be chosen to compete in St. Louis for the Olympics. He was there for Mary Elisha, not to garner praise for his athletic accomplishments.

CHICAGO - 1904

Early in the year, Ray had been invited to compete for the USA in the upcoming Olympic Games. Because Nelle hadn't seen her parents since the wedding in 1900 and there was no time to visit them after Mary Elisha's funeral, the Ewry's decided to visit Nelle's father's new home in Chicago before Ray would travel south to Washington University in St. Louis for the Olympic Games.

Ray and Nelle arrived in Chicago a week before the Games. They had been there but two days when Nelle, realizing Ray was getting anxious to get to St. Louis, cut him loose. He felt bad about leaving so quickly after arriving but knew she was right. He needed to flush everything from his mind and focus on the upcoming Games.

The 1903 World's Fair had been set to take place in Chicago, but due to insurmountable construction delays, the event was rescheduled for St. Louis in 1904. James E. Sullivan, the Director of the Olympic Games, upon hearing of the date and venue change, lobbied to have the Olympics added to the St. Louis venue.

Mr. Sullivan, the consummate marketer, wanted these Olympics to excel and used all his political capital to have the Games recognized as truly a "world event". On April 30, 1904, President Theodore Roosevelt pressed a telegraphic device in Washington, D.C. that signaled the opening of the Exposition, and once again, the Games were associated with the World's Fair, also known as "The Louisiana Purchase Exposition".

Unfortunately, the Exposition mirrored the confusing timeline of the Paris Games in 1900. To make matters worse, James E. Sullivan wanted all the sporting events scheduled from May 14 through December 1 to be considered Olympic in nature, even including interscholastic events and non-Olympic sports.

For Olympic purists, the track and field events were held from August 29 through September 3. These events were the subject of most of the nation's newspapers, as the other events were considered mere "championships".

In preparation for the Olympic Games, the campus of Washington University saw many newly constructed buildings and a new track built to accommodate the Exposition's track and field events. The track was a $1/3^{rd}$ of a mile oval that allowed the 100 and 200-meter dashes to be held on lined lanes down the straightaway. These individual lanes prevented any interference claims as happened in the two prior Olympics.

To ensure speedy results for the 400 and 800-meter events, the track was built 20 feet wide, thus allowing most events to be contested in one heat. The infield where the weight throwing events were held was marked by lines in an ever-widening semi-circle going out in one direction away from the throwing circle.

All these innovations were greatly appreciated by the athletes who had participated in the mass confusion of the Bois de Boulogne in Paris.

Thanks to James E. Sullivan, who planned the entire layout, the appreciative spectators sitting in the stands, or gathered along the bordering grassy areas around the field, were delighted to be able to see the track and field events without having to trek across the campus to view the various events.

Before the Games, the organizing committee was concerned about the socio-political scene of Europe due to the Russo-Japanese war. So far, only 12 countries had sent athletes to the campus of Washington University[14].

---

[14] The total number of registered competitors reached 630, with most of them coming from the U.S.

31

ST. LOUIS – The Louisiana Purchase Exposition - 1904

Ray arrived in St. Louis on August 11th and immediately went to the Washington University campus to find his quarters and settle into the disciplined routine he had applied in Paris. He felt very confident that by the time the track and field events were to take place, from August 29th through September 3rd, he would have plenty of time to become familiar with the grounds and get into top competitive form.

He ran into Martin Sheridan and some old friends and competitors from the Paris Games watching the opening parade and the first day of preliminary heats. Meyer Prinstein, Archie Hahn, James Lightbody, Harry Hillman and Ray stood together and were intrigued as they watched the competition between "tribal" men from Patagonia, the Philippines, Japan, Africa, Mexico, and even a contingent of Native American Indians.

These multi-racial events were the reason these games were called the "Anthropology Days". The first Africans ever to compete in the Olympic Games were two Zulu tribesmen, Yamasani and Lentauw. They were part of the Boer War exhibit at the Exposition and were last-minute entrants in the marathon.

Ray and his fellow teammates were captivated by the events of August 13th and 14th when the Department of Anthology sponsored the competition between members of the tribes who were in St. Louis to be part of their country's Physical Culture exhibits.

Each tribe, as they were called, held competitions for specified events among themselves and then brought the first and second place winners out for a tribal competition to determine the overall winners.

The spectacle was both praised by scientific researchers and scorned by many spectators and many minor players in the organizations that supported the World's Fair as inhumane.

The events held at Washington University's Francis Field were as follows: 100-yard dash, 440-yard run, 16-lb. shotput, 120-yard hurdles, 1-mile run, 100-meter dash, running broad jump, running high jump, throwing bolos, throwing a baseball, 56-lb. weight throw, accuracy throw, javelin throw, pole climb, archery and finally the tug-of-war.

That day the American athletes noted that there seemed to be more academic and scientific observers documenting the results of each heat of each event than mere spectators, and they weren't far off. The one constant that carried over from the 1896 and 1900 Olympics was the "team" concept as opposed to one United States Olympic Team.

Each athletic club had its athletes wear the insignia of the club. Ray and the other past medalists had come to St. Louis, not as a unified American team, but to compete against the best in the world for their individual clubs, universities, and colleges.

Once they learned how few countries would be competing, they realized that the Games would be a glorified Club Championship.

Most of the athletes from the competing New York Athletic Club, the Chicago Athletic Association, the Greater New York Irish-American Athletic Association, the Milwaukee Athletic Club, and the host Missouri Athletic Club were interested more in winning the massive A.G. Spaulding trophy presented to the winning team. At the end of the club competition, the NYAC won the coveted Spaulding Trophy.

The fear of redundancy looms large when it comes to recounting Ray's events of the 1904 Olympic Games. He never wavered from his pre-jump routine and due to his reputation as the best standing jumper in the world, the crowd of spectators grew three-fold.

Since more than a dozen athletes were entered in each of the standing jumping events, they had to perform three qualifying jumps to trim the field down and establish the top three competitors for the medals round.

Once the final three had been determined, the top three competitors were afforded a one-hour respite, then escorted back to the high jump location. For the medals round, the final three athletes were obliged to compete in three more jumps to determine the first, second, and third place winners.

On August 29th, the first day of the formal track and field competition, Ray was in perfect form for the standing broad jump. He bettered his own world's record by an inch, reaching 11.4 feet & 7/8th inches (3.47 meters), breaking the existing Olympic record. Ray's jump bested Charles King's second-place attempt by over 7 inches and John Biller's bronze medal jump of 10 feet 8 ¼ inches.

On August 30th, Martin Sheridan happened to see a Cuban competitor, Felix Carbajal deSoto, waiting for the start of the marathon in heavy street shoes, long pants, and a long-sleeve shirt. Martin found out that deSoto had lost all his clothing and travel monies gambling in New Orleans and had to hitch-hike to St. Louis.

The temperature was approaching 90 degrees and Martin knew the Cuban, although used to warm weather, would be hard-pressed to finish in the heat wearing his heavy clothes.

Martin found a pair of scissors and proceeded to trim the runner's pant legs and long sleeves. Although the trimming of his cumbersome clothing helped, Felix finished the 24.85-mile distance in fourth place, just under four hours.

August 31st brought new athletes into the standing high jump competition and on this date, Ray met his first black challenger, Joseph Stadler, from Cleveland, Ohio.

As usual, the three preliminary jumps per athlete were performed, thus eliminating all but the top three jumpers, notably Ray Ewry with 5.3 feet (1.60 meters), Joseph Stadler with 4.9 feet (1.44 meters), and Lawson Robertson, who tied Stadler with 4.9 feet (1.44 meters) jump.

Since the two men had tied, they were forced into a "jump off" which Stadler won. To the chagrin of some of the athletes, Ray was quick to congratulate Stadler on his second-place finish.

As August rolled into September, the third event in Ray's schedule was set to take place on the third day of the month. Ray and the competing athletes performed their obligatory three qualifying attempts for the standing triple jump medals.

After all the athletes had jumped, the top three leaders for the finals were Ray Ewry, Charles King, and again, Joseph Stadler.

Martin Sheridan, Ray's best friend, came over to the group waiting for the official's signal for the final jumps and asked for Ray's best wishes as he was about to go up against the 6-foot 6 inch, 265-pound gentle giant, Ralph Rose in the discus throw.

Martin was intimidated by Rose who had broken the world's record in the shot put with a toss of the amazing distance of 48 feet 7 inches.

Ray put an arm around his friend and asked him to wait until this final jump was concluded, then he would go with him to his event location on the field and cheer him on. That seemed to settle Martin down.

Ray, King, and Stadler went one after another and at the end of their three final jumps, the results below were written into the record books.

Ray Ewry - Gold – 34.7 & ¼ feet (10.54 meters)

Charles King – Silver – 33.4 feet (10.16 meters)

Joseph Stadler – Bronze – 31.6 feet (9.60 meters)

The discus throw was a very popular event at the 1904 Games, as it was one of the events that spanned the centuries, from the ancient Olympics in Athens to the present.

The throwing circle for the discus was the center of the universe for these competitors. The elimination rounds were the same for the discus, with the athletes making three qualifying throws. The three longest throws went head to head for the medals round.

At the end of six throws, Ralph Rose and Martin Sheridan were tied with equal throws of 128.10 & ½ feet. Abiding by the rules of competition for these Games, the officials called for one more set of three throws to determine the champion.

Martin was chosen to go first and after the second round of throws, Rose had the longest toss so far. Even though Martin Sheridan was 6 feet 3 inches, Ralph Rose seemed to tower over him, laughing as Martin went into Ray's bizarre crouch to focus on his last attempt.

The official decided to flip a coin for the order of throws and Rose had to go first. Both men were exhausted from the previous eight throws and as Rose entered the circle, Martin gave Ray a forlorn look.

Rose began his technique with the standard three half-body twists, went into the pre-throw 360-degree body spin, and launched the discus down the field for what most of the spectators assumed would be the winning mark.

Martin's head dropped as he saw an official place a small flag in the grass at the exact landing point and the distance of 120 feet 6 and ¾ inches was marked on the chalkboard.

It was now Martin's turn and he took his discus from the official, stepped into the circle, and stood absolutely still; his head bowed in concentration. Finally, he performed the standard three half-body twists and began his 360-degree body spin. As he let the discus go, he let out a roar of exertion that sounded like a wounded lion, startling everyone close to the circle.

The discus sailed toward the curved lines in the grass and slammed into the soft ground at the astonishing mark of 127.10 & ¼ feet.

When the distance was marked and recorded, Martin was victorious and everyone who saw the gold medal-winning throw erupted in thunderous cheers.

A serious black mark on the Games was caused by Fred Lorz who, in the 40k marathon, decided to hop in a car and be driven most of the distance. He jumped out of the vehicle a short distance from the stadium and finished the race in first place to the roar of the unsuspecting crowd in the stadium. When the hoax was discovered and passed the eventual winner, Thomas Hicks was declared the winner.

Fred Lorz was banned from all amateur competition for life; but a year later, the ban was lifted in time for him to come in first in the 1905 Boston marathon.

When the events of the "Anthropology Days" competitions were disclosed to Baron de Coubertin, he commented that the efforts of the Olympic movement had again been overshadowed by a larger venue, namely the 1900 Paris Exposition and now the 1904 World's Fair.

He felt that the Americans brought the "Anthropology Days" into the fabric of the Exposition to prove the athletic superiority of the "white man" over the indigenous tribes from the various cultures that had originally been set up to display their individual villages and their habits of every-day life.

In the end, the 1904 St. Louis Olympics proved to be a success by some, but most saw it as a failure for de Coubertin supporters and their view of what the Olympics should have been.

The ultimate winners in track and field were Archie Hahn, Harry Hillman, James Lightbody and Ray Ewry. These four athletes had each won three individual gold medals and were the "darlings" of the media.

The 1904 Games also provided America with its first black athletes, Joseph Stadler and more notably George Poage who went on to win two bronze medals in both the 200 and 400-meter hurdles.

Another first was the entry of the Native American Indian, Frank Pierce into the marathon.

The New York Athletic Club narrowly defeated the Chicago Athletic Association for overall team points. The CAA. They charged the NYAC with planting a "ringer" in their line-up for the tug-of-war, but the outcome went to the NYAC "winged foot" team, as did the coveted Spaulding trophy.

BALTIMORE - 1990

Olympic Stars

1. Ray Ewry recovered from paralysis to win 10 Olympic gold medals between 1900 and 1908. One of the all-time great jumpers, Ewry's wins came in the standing high-, long-, and triple-jump events; in 1904, he set a world record of 11 feet 4⅞ inches in the standing long jump, which he held until the event was discontinued in 1936.

In 1990, I was contacted by a representative of the United States Postal Service regarding a request for permission to publish a U.S. stamp of Ray's iconic image as he vaulted over the high bar. It was quite an honor to have Ray chosen to be among the five Olympic athletes for the series.

I asked why the Postal Service felt Ray and the other four honored athletes would be a successful venture and was told that there had been many requests by collectors to feature Olympians. The postal official thought that after a few years Ray's stamp and the four other honored athlete's stamps might be worth quite a lot of money to collectors of Olympic memorabilia. This statement ignited my curiosity again.

Still, without a computer, I went to the local library and researched coin and stamp collectors and was amazed to find it to be a very large international community and it could be very lucrative.

I also found some local collectors of Olympic memorabilia and looked them up. When contacted, most of them were vague about authentic Olympic gold medals, almost to a suspicious level, as if they didn't want an outsider probing too deeply into their world. They did say to keep an eye out for any collector's showcases coming to the Maryland-Virginia area in the future.

33

NEW YORK CITY - 1906

On a rainy evening in early April, Ray and Nelle had been driven to a friend's brownstone a few blocks from Central Park. Ray told the driver to wait for him as he walked Nelle to the front door and greeted their friends. Ray kissed Nelle farewell and climbed back into the Hansom and headed for the New York Athletic Club.

At 7:30 p.m., thirty-four elite athletes entered the main boardroom. The United States Olympic Committee had called this meeting to formally welcome the athletes who had been chosen to represent the United States in the 10th anniversary of the Modern Olympics for the 1906 Olympics in Athens, Greece. The Club president, Mr. John H. Van Wormer, gave a spirited speech praising the athletes, ending it with the toast, "God speed!"

James Sullivan, the secretary of the powerful AAU[15], was more to the point and informed the athletes that Mr. Matthew "Matty" Halpin would be acting as the team manager while en route to Greece and throughout the Games.

Sullivan implored them to observe the same good sportsmanship they displayed during the 1904 St. Louis Games. He also informed them that they would no longer be allowed to wear the emblems of their clubs on their tunics. To squelch the large egos of some, all would be displaying the United States Olympic team emblem.

It was impressed upon each that they represented the United States as a team. Sullivan lamented the fact that many great collegiate athletes were not able to break free of their obligations at school and could not make the trip but was very confident that the team assembled before him would do the USA proud. He raised a glass and uttered the toast, "Victory!"

---

[15] The American Athletic Union

After the cheers of the athletes subsided, he introduced "Matty" Halpin, who approached the head of the table, greeted them warmly, and introduced a uniformed Captain Langreuther from the North German Lloyd Line.

Captain Langreuther told the team he was looking forward to seeing them at the Hoboken, New Jersey dock tomorrow morning, the 3rd of April, at 10 a.m. sharp. After loading their belongings, the vessel named "*S.S. Barbarossa*" would leave at 11 a.m.

He also informed the team that he had arranged for the crew to build a temporary training track on the massive deck of the vessel. This news brought the team to their feet with a round of applause and loud cheers.

Behind the Captain, a large map of the Atlantic Ocean and Europe outlined the trip they were about to take. With a long pointer, the Captain traced the voyage from Hoboken, across the Atlantic Ocean, and through the Straights of Gibraltar to the Italian port of Naples.

After landing, the team would board a train for the southeastern port of Brindizi, sail to the Grecian port of Patras and proceed to Athens by train.

In his journal on the 1906 Olympic Games, Ray wrote that the Captain was asked about the mid-March eruption of Mount Vesuvius that was so close to Naples. The Captain said that the railways were undamaged as the flow was on the southern edge of the volcano, away from Naples.

When "Matty" Halpin and Captain Langreuther returned to their seats, James Sullivan returned to the head of the table. He opened an official envelope with the Presidential seal and read an inspirational letter from President Theodore "Teddy" Roosevelt. Sullivan concluded the meeting by informing the team he would rendezvous with them in Naples, Italy en route to Athens.

34

HOBOKEN, NEW JERSEY - 1906

For the first time since the 1896 Olympic Games in Athens, athletes' wives were permitted to travel with their husbands, but only if they could pay for the added portage on their own.

As the *"S.S. Barbarossa"* backed away from the pier, thousands of family members, sports supporters, and well-wishers cheered and waved farewell.

From the ship's log, the first day of the voyage across the Atlantic was uneventful. The second day started out calm and sunny but changed to darkening skies and ever-increasing winds. Many of the athletes were circling the makeshift track the Captain had erected as the storm approached. Most everyone heeded the deck hand's suggestion that they go below until the storm passed, but machismo was evident, as some stayed on deck.

Only a few crewmembers saw the ominous rolling rogue wave as it bore down on the starboard side of the vessel and had no time to warn anyone. When it slammed into the side of the ship, everyone was thrown to the deck as the ship listed to the port side.

When the ocean settled, and the damage assessments were completed, the Captain had to inform the shaken passengers of some tragic news. There were a few missing crewmembers who must have been swept overboard and two deaths from head injuries from the ship's manifest of regular passengers.

At dinner that night, the Ewrys and the Edgrens listened in shock to many stories of the rogue wave event. A long-distance runner for the American team, Harvey Cohn, was saved from being swept overboard by the quick reactions of the diver, Frank Bornamann, who injured himself as he dove across the deck just as Cohn was hit by the wall of ocean water.

Ray's NYAC fellow athlete and world champion hurdler, Harry Hillman, injured a knee so badly that he wasn't able to compete in the Athens Games.

Another story circulated about Herbert Kerrigan and Martin Sheridan, who were slightly injured as both were slammed up against the steel wall of the main deck lounge. Getting the worst from the violent wave was James Mitchel, a weight thrower, who dislocated a shoulder. It was thought that Mitchel was in contention for a gold medal in several events, but the injury put a cloud over his chances to compete.

The remainder of the voyage was uneventful and on April 13th the "*S.S. Barbarossa*" docked at the port of Gibraltar for supplies but found very little to load on board due to the volcanic eruption of Mount Vesuvius a week earlier.

With the food supplies being rationed, Nelle Ewry and Mrs. Bob Edgren hatched a plan to leave the ship and gather food from the street markets. Once they realized U.S. currency would be of no use to them, they came up with an idea on how to pay the vendors for the needed supplies.

The two adventurous ladies took two large baskets each and ventured into the Gibraltar marketplace armed with trinkets and personal belongings to use as bartering tools.

They spent all morning stopping at various market stalls trading hats, clothing, jewelry, and anything the merchants and their wives might want in exchange for roasting chickens, fresh lamb, and copious amounts of fresh vegetables. This was the first venture of what was to become "The Ladies Auxiliary Society", which functioned throughout the 1906 Olympic schedule. Without the Society's efforts, the athletes would never have had the proper protein and nutritional foods to keep them in competitive form.

Once the "*S.S. Barbarossa*" docked in Naples on the 16th of April, the passengers who had looked forward to seeing Naples were alarmed at the condition of the post-eruption city. They saw the beautiful landscape covered with a thin layer of gray volcanic ash and most of the citizens holding handkerchiefs or cloth up to their faces.

As the passengers were loaded onto wagons to be transported to the train station, a team of Italian customs agents came on board and began to inspect the ship's supplies. When they entered one of the storage compartments near the main galley, they saw labeled cases of White Rock bottled "mineral water" stacked against one wall.

Without even tasting the water, they ordered a squad of Italian soldiers to confiscate the cases and unload them onto the dock. As a large horse-drawn wagon was being loaded with the cases, "Matty" Halpin confronted the leader of the customs squad and demanded that he, or someone...anyone from his squad, sample the contents.

Through an interpreter, Halpin learned that the agent believed the clear liquid in the bottles to be American-made "gin". He declared the liquid to be illegal to import into Italy and terminated the conversation.

Matty Halpin was so enraged by the officer's inability to compromise he stormed off declaring his intention to lodge a formal complaint with local officials.

Later, the chief customs official, fearing a government reprimand, replaced the so-called "gin" with an equal amount of light Italian wine, since there was very little potable water available in the city due to the eruption of Vesuvius.

The American athletes thought they could practice on dry land but soon found that the two to three inches of volcanic dust made it virtually impossible, but they labored on until they grew tired of breathing in the dust.

Bob Edgren and Ray were so curious about the volcano they decided not to practice. They hired a local man to cart them the distance from the port to the base of the volcano, then ascended the 1300 meters of cooling magma to peer into the smoking caldera.

Ray noted in his journal that they could only stay for a few minutes as the noxious gasses and heat were too much for them, but at least they returned with a great story of being right on the edge of the rim.

When Ray told Nelle of his little adventure, she was quite upset with his recklessness. She forbade him to wander away from her ever again.

As the train left Naples, the passengers were awe-struck as they passed within a few miles of the site of the eruption. They saw the dark plume of smoke and ash rising a mile above Mount Vesuvius and all were happy to make the trip to Brindizi and clean fresh air.

Once they arrived in Brindizi and began to load their belongings onto the smaller steamship *"Montenegro"* for the short voyage to Patras, the "Ladies Auxiliary" again ventured into the marketplace to gather supplies.

They even managed to coerce a water-delivery wagon driver to amend his daily schedule to unload ten five-gallon jugs of water on the dock in trade for three pairs of dress shoes from various athletes.

"From all accounts, Mrs. Nelle Ewry and Mrs. Bob Edgren, having amassed a fair amount of nourishing foods, cooked a fabulous meal for the entire team and coaches on the Greek Isle of Corfu. It turned out to be the best part of the extremely difficult and exhausting trip so far."

New York Times – 1906

35

ATHENS – April 1906

After the 215-kilometer train ride from Patras to Athens, the athletes were tired and happy to finally come to the end of their long journey. They were welcomed by the Greek organizing committee and escorted to their living quarters.

To the chagrin of the athletes and their wives, the accommodations were found to be Spartan at best. Many large exhibition halls had been transformed into temporary housing by erecting small, curtained cubicles for sleeping that offered little privacy, much less a quiet night's sleep. Ray, Bob Edgren, and Martin Sheridan, having seen the athlete's accommodations, were aided by a local guide and promptly booked rooms at the Hermes Hotel.

On the 19th, the restaurant next to the hotel was filled with concerned Americans as they learned about the San Francisco earthquake and subsequent fire that ravaged the city. Many rushed to the one telegraph office they knew of and fired off requests for more information about the devastating tragedy.

The alarming news from America must have made the team somewhat testy because, after three days of being fed rubbery goat meat, the American team revolted and caused quite a scene as they refused to eat the meals set before them. To a man, they left their quarters and booked rooms in the Hermes as well.

April 22

Athletes from around the world assembled in the open plaza outside the newly renovated Panathenaic Stadium in preparation for the opening ceremonies.

As each country lined up its athletes for the grand entrance, they were asked to open their ranks to allow a procession of horse-drawn carriages to drive through.

Only a few of the athletes recognized the occupants, but when they saw the British and Greek athletes applauding as the carriages passed by, they realized there was royalty entering the stadium ahead of them.

The first carriage in the procession carried King Georgios and his sister, Queen Alexandra of Great Britain, while the second carried Greek Queen Olga and her brother-in-law, King Edward the VII, also of Great Britain, and the Prince and Princess of Wales.

In the plaza, each team member was issued an identity pin; basically an "all-access" event pass. They were told that for the first time in the modern Olympic era, they would be marching into the stadium one after another and to position their flag-bearer at the front of each national team for the 80,000 spectators to recognize the representation of their mother country.

Inside the stadium, the dignitaries seated in the royal box listened to Crown Prince Konstantinos as he petitioned the King of Greece to proclaim the opening of the Games of Athens. Once the King declared the opening, the parade of athletes began.

Per Dr. Bill Mallon's comprehensive book, *"History of the Early Olympics, 4 - The 1906 Olympic Games"*, the order of countries that entered the stadium was not set up in alphabetical order, but is thought to have been as follows:

Germany, United States, Great Britain, Sweden, France, Italy, Belgium, Denmark, Norway, Austria, Hungary, Finland, Egypt, Switzerland, and finally Greece.

As the American flag-bearer, Matthew "Matty" Halpin, passed by the royal booth, he dipped the flag for the first time in a show of respect to the dignitaries and the King of Greece.

After the parade of nations, the competition began with male and female athletes treating the spectators and the balance of athletes to a stimulating display of gymnastics by Denmark, Sweden, and Greece.

April 25

The fourth day of competition proved golden for Ray and Martin Sheridan, as both men excelled in their chosen events. Martin broke the world's record for the discus with his final toss of 41.46 meters (136.02 feet) and Ray dominated the standing broad jump by starting with a distance of 3.15 meters (10.33 feet). After two more attempts, he secured first place with a final leap of 3.30 meters (10.83 feet).

While practicing the standing broad jump, Martin landed badly and injured his right leg, but still managed to place second with a leap of 3.095 meters (10.15 feet). After the event, Martin confided in Ray about his injury and both realized he would probably not be able to enter the pentathlon competition.

For an athlete who was considered one of the greatest all-around competitors in the world, this was quite a blow.

Since Ray wasn't competing until the first of May, he and Nelle toured many historical sites in Athens and made daily excursions to surrounding cities and ports.

Ray wrote that Nelle, no matter how beautiful the view or impressive the ancient ruins were, would constantly seek and barter for nutritional food for the close group of athletes and wives back at the hotel.

May 1

On the final day of the track and field competition, the most popular event as far as the Greeks were concerned was the running of the marathon. After the marathon runners had left the stadium, Ray and Martin were entered in the standing high jump. Martin and another American, Lawson Robertson, tied with a Belgian jumper, Leon DuPont, with a final elevation of the bar set at 1.40 meters (4.49 feet).

Ray finished out the competition by attempting to set a new world record with the bar set at 1.66 meters (5.45 feet), but he failed at that height and settled for his gold medal jump of 5.12 feet (1.56 meters).

With Ray's final jump of the 1906 Athens Olympics, he had won eight Olympic firsts and was considered by all Olympic aficionados as the greatest standing jumper in the world.

May 2

At the awards ceremonies, when Ray's name was called, he stepped up to the royal's booth and bowed respectfully as King Georgios placed an olive wreath from the sacred Altis in Olympia on his head, two gold medals around his neck, and honored his efforts by handing him two engraved trophies.[16]

Of all the accolades heaped upon Ray during the Games in Athens, the one that registered the most was the gift from Crown Prince Konstantinos of a large Grecian urn.

---

[16] On page 57 in the "*From Vision to Victory*", an NYAC special edition for the Games of the XXVIII Olympiad in Athens Greece, Ray is pictured holding these exact trophies. The notation below the picture states that he won four of these trophies. Two of them were returned to me in 1980 and are now are now part of the private Ewry memorabilia collection. The whereabouts of the other two trophies is unknown.

The urn Ray described in his journal had hand-painted images depicting athletes in various modes of competition, but the true value of the gift was the urn's content. It was filled with the hallowed soil from the ancient Greek stadium.

May 3

On the last day of the Athens Olympics, team manager Halpin had to collect all the members of the American Olympic team for a group photo requested by President Teddy Roosevelt.

As the Acropolis glowed orange behind him, King Georgios gave many speeches at the final royal reception that night. He was exhilarated with the results of the efforts of all his fellow countrymen in restoring the majesty and pride of the Olympics and of Athens itself; he offered a toast followed by a speech to all the athletes, wives, and foreign dignitaries.

"Greece, who has been the mother and nurse of the Olympic Games in ancient times and who had undertaken to celebrate them once more today, can now hope, as their success has gone beyond all expectations, will remember Athens as the peaceful meeting place of all nations, as the tranquil and permanent seat of the Olympics."

On their last day in Athens, Ray rented a carriage and had the driver take them to the Coliseum so he could take a picture of the famous building. Later that night, the Ewry's were taken up to the Parthenon.

As he and Nelle stood near one of the most iconic structures in the world and looked out over the beautiful ancient city, Ray reached into his jacket pocket and offered a thick envelope to her.

Inside the envelope were "paid-for" travel vouchers for several countries in Europe. Ray had purchased them as a wedding present.

He explained to Nelle that ever since their wedding in 1900 their lives had been too busy to take a prolonged honeymoon. With his new position with the Navy and his participation in the last three Olympics, they hadn't had time for anything else.

So, as the U.S. Olympians sailed back to the United States, Ray and Nelle began their honeymoon. They spent the next two months traveling throughout Europe and the British Isles.

A month after his return from the 1906 Athens Olympics, Ray was approached by a high-ranking member of the New York City Board of Water Supply. He was looking for a talented engineer to assume the newly created post of Assistant Mechanical Engineer for the new Catskill Aqueduct Project.

This meant that Ray would be the on-site director of the massive project to design and supervise the construction of the dams and underground aqueducts needed to boost the water supply to New York City.

In his journal, Ray wrote that he was interviewed for over two hours. Unfortunately, he wasn't allowed to give sensitive details about his six years of employment with the U.S. Navy other than to list his accomplishments.

Ray was the Chief Engineer for the completion of the U.S. cruiser "*Chattanooga*", Chief Engineer for the completion of the U.S. torpedo boats "*Nicholson*" and "*O'Brien*" and Chief Engineer for steam work on the new battleship "*New York*".

Within a week, Ray was offered the lucrative position and gave his notice to his superiors at the Naval Yard. On the last day of his employ, a large farewell dinner was held in his honor.

Shortly after his career change, Ray volunteered to be part of a fund-raising event to support the earthquake-damaged Non-Sectarian Orphan House in San Francisco.

The event was staged at New York's American League Park, and to the delight of the spectators, Ray broke the existing world's record for the standing broad jump by leaping the never before attained distance of 11'6", but after the judges noticed a depression in the ground and declared the jump invalid.

After Ray settled into his New York City office at the Board of Water Supply and became familiar with the demands of his new position, he was sent to the Catskills in western New York State to begin work on the Ashokan Dam Project.

DOUGLAS MANOR – Long Island, New York - 1906

After the wonderful year, they had spent preparing for the Athens Games and their subsequent European "honeymoon" tour, the Ewry's moved into their new home and life returned to normal. Ray had taken a few weeks off from training after returning to America and in late September, he resumed his training in the small backyard of their home.

During the ensuing years between the Olympics, Ray spent many hours in the NYAC training facility at the Central Park South location and the Travers Island complex. His technique, which had been copied since the 1900 Paris Games, was still perfect, but Ray quietly noted that his distances were beginning to diminish. His fellow athletes watched him do his specialty jumps and noticed the drop but said nothing to the world record holder.

At the age of 35, most athletes were considered "over the hill", but Ray was still a dedicated competitor and all his fellow club members marveled at his stamina and focus as he set the standard for training ethics.

At home, Nelle noticed that Ray spent more time massaging his knees and ankles in the steaming water in their bathtub after a training session. When she asked him how he was doing, he would reply that he was just a little stiff.

Arthritis was creeping into his joints, but as Ray had done all his life, he approached the restrictive physical effects by doing anything it took to get his body to obey his commands.

Sadly, on January 26th, Nelle's mother passed away from a relapse while visiting relatives in Lafayette. When the ominous telegram arrived, Nelle and Ray again boarded a train for Lafayette. They arrived too late to attend the services held at Dr. Davidson's residence but could make it to Springvale Cemetery for the interment service.

Ray wrote that his love for Nelle grew even deeper as he watched her take control of the maudlin situation and made sure that all the loved ones and friends focused on her mother's charitable and compassionate life instead of mourning their loss of such a beloved woman.

The Ewry's stayed for three more days to wrap up matters and afterward, accompanied Mr. Johnson back to his home in Chicago before returning to New York.

LONDON - 1908

Shortly after the 1906 Olympics had come to a close, the disappointed Italian contingent in charge of planning the 1908 Rome Olympics informed the I.O.C. officials that due to the Mount Vesuvius eruption and the devastation to Naples, the funds set aside for the Games would have to be channeled into aid for the city's infrastructure repair.

Knowing the Games were scheduled to begin in two years, the IOC scrambled to find a suitable location. When they learned that Lord Desborough, who had competed for England on the fencing team, was still lounging on the fencing team's yacht in Piraeus harbor, they informed him of their thoughts of a London Olympics in two years.

When Lord Desborough returned to England, he spoke with King Edward VII, who had also attended the Athens Games. The King was amenable to the idea, but only if the newly formed British Olympic Association (BOA) had the promise of financial assistance from the British government.

In November of 1906, after many negotiations, confirming news spread that London would indeed host the 1908 Olympic Games. The location of the Games would be Shepherd's Bush, London.

ATHLETICS. —R. C. EWRY (U.S.A.) WINNING THE
STANDING HIGH JUMP.

SHEPHERD'S BUSH

For over 800 years, shepherds transporting their cattle, horses, and swine stopped at the wooded "common land" plot that in the later years was called "Shepherd's Bush". It was the main resting point before reaching the famous Smithfield Market in London.

In 1860, Parliament established the "Metropolitan Meat and Poultry Market Act" which permanently closed the vile-smelling plot due to its proximity to London. The operation was moved to the current Charterhouse Street location, leaving "Shepherd's Bush" vacant.

Mr. Imre Kiralfy, the Director-General of the Franco-British Exposition, was a man of vision and capable of producing wonderfully vibrant exhibitions around the world. Years before, he had a vision of a grand "White City" on the unused site of Shepherd's Bush for the Franco-British Exposition set for 1908.

The IOC, fearing the same dismal results of pairing the 1900 and 1904 Games with World's Fairs, made provisions that protected the 1908 Olympics from being over-shadowed.

When Lord Desborough returned from Athens in 1906, he and Kiralfy met and devised a plan to add a spectacular new stadium into the architectural plans for the Exposition. Kiralfy knew immediately that if he could bring the Olympics into an equal association with the Franco-British Exposition it would only improve the attraction of the athletic spectacle. After many meetings, the plan was accepted and construction began.

Once the stadium was completed, the track that Charles Perry had designed was touted as "the greatest track in the world'. The spectator's stands surrounded a 300' x 700' banked oval concrete track for the cycling events, a one-third of a mile cinder track, a 100-meter swimming pool built directly in front of the royal boxes, and a massive grass infield that would be the venue for all the field events. The stadium offered seating for 63,000 spectators and standing room for another 30,000.

In early July, the American contingent sailed from New York, destined for Southampton, England with high hopes of capturing a majority of gold medals. The line-up of athletes for the various events was regarded as "world-class" by most of the national and international press. The London Olympics began to look as though they would become a battle for national supremacy between the U.S.A. and England.

Remembering the dismal accommodations offered the athletes and their wives in Athens, James Sullivan arranged for the team to be housed in the southern coastal resort town of Brighton, some 53 miles south of London.[17] The American team was scheduled to be shuttled to the Olympic stadium and back to Brighton each day by train.

On the 11th of July, the American athletes and coaches were invited to attend the formal reception for Olympians from every country.

Ray wrote that he was very impressed with the way the British Olympic Committee presented a preview of the Games during the banquet.

Even though the 1906 Games in Athens had its share of royal pageantry, the London Olympics staged formal "opening ceremonies". Both national and international dignitaries, along with ranking officers from the British military, joined the King and Queen of England and their children in the Royal boxes. In the adjacent boxes on both sides of the royal family, dignitaries from all the competing countries were seated.

On the cold, rainy afternoon of July 13th, once Baron de Coubertin had introduced the International Olympic Committee to the King, Lord Desborough petitioned the King to declare the 1908 Olympic Games in London to be opened.

The King stood behind a lavish, twenty-foot Persian rug and before a hushed audience he said,

"I declare the Olympic Games of London open!"

---

[17] No references have been found about wives accompanying their husbands to the London Olympics.

With his declaration, one of the most hotly contested Olympics in the Modern Era began.

All the participating countries entered in the London Olympics were excited to compete, especially after reading the new regulations and guidelines established by the IOC; all except the English and Irish athletes.

There are quite a few opinions as to the origin of the schism between the two countries. One refers to the 1108 invasion when the English killed many Irish leaders and placed a ban on learning to read and write and implemented the penalty of death for anyone who set up schools to teach those basic skills.

Another opinion focuses on Henry VIII and his wife, Catherine of Aragon, who gave birth to Mary I. After many miscarriages and stillbirths, Henry, realizing no suitable male heir would come from the marriage, requested the Catholic Church give him an annulment. When his request was denied, he established the Church of England and began persecuting any Irish citizens who wouldn't recognize or convert to his church.

Unfortunately, the deep wounds from past atrocities and the ever-present animosity caused by their religious differences over the centuries bubbled just under the surface as the London Olympics began.

The majority of Olympic athletes from the NYAC were Irish and along with the great athletes from the Irish-American Athletic Club, there was a high level of mistrust and paranoia about the fairness of the host country's judging at the Games.

Lest we forget, there was also a deep-rooted resentment on the part of many British citizens regarding the fact that many years before, the "Yanks" had defeated England during the American Revolution.

This established their freedom from British rule. The table was set for what Olympic historians called "The Battle of Shepherd's Bush".

The Edwardian British athletes were intent on displaying their sporting superiority to the rest of the world, whereas the arrogant American upstarts were focused on proving that they were indeed "world-class" athletes and were anxious to compete against the Brits on the Olympic stage.

As soon as the opening ceremonies began, the Swedes and Americans noticed when viewing the vast display of national flags that ringed the stadium, that their country's standards were absent.

The team from Finland, which was considered part of Russia, marched without a flag as their request to carry the Finnish flag was denied by the mother country. Even though they were not included on the official list of nations entered in the Olympics, the fact that the flags of Japan and China were displayed only added to the insult.

The Americans considered their missing "Old Glory" a public snub and thus, when the flag bearer, Ralph Rose, passed by the Royal Box of the King and Queen, he refused to exhibit the proper protocol as all other nations had by dipping their national flags.

To the shock of the Brits, Rose kept the "stars and stripes" in a vertical position. Not much was made of the incident until Martin Sheridan was quoted as saying, *"This flag dips to no earthly king!"*

Letter from Ray to Nelle – July 15, 1908

My dearest girl,

London just isn't the same without my beautiful Nelle. The weather is as dismal as we remembered when we made our way back home from the Athens trip. There is always the threat of rain and cool winds to dampen the spirit.

Martin and I share a comfortable room with full amenities in a small hotel in Brighton. We have been training on the beach pebbles and I find that I get no firm footing for my practice takeoffs. My knees and hips are becoming somewhat sore and swell if I don't stretch afterward they tend to tighten up. Luckily, there is a wonderful hot-water bath that I have grown to enjoy immensely after the training and it helps with the soreness.

The opening of the spectacle took place two days ago with the whole team ablaze with anger and resentment toward the Brits who failed to include Old Glory in the opening day's festivities. No doubt the Swedes were incensed at finding their flag was also missing from the display.

As we entered the stadium, the sight of all the national flags ringing the stands was at first quite impressive until an ominous feeling overtook us as we marched toward the King and Queen's location. It seemed we all took note that our flag was missing at the same time.

As we passed the reviewing stand, there were no smiles or any signs of jubilation from us. I didn't notice it at the time, but I'm told we did not adhere to international protocol and dip our flag concerning the Royals, and that seems to have angered the local dignitaries and the British spectators.

Besides the competition, I have been looking forward to viewing the various booths and displays at the Franco-British Exposition. I'm told that a few of us will be able to visit, but I'll have to wait and see.

I hope all is well on the home front. I know you are holding strong and you must know that immediately after the competition I will be returning home on the first vessel departing Southampton. I am taking good care not to over-extend myself.

Hopefully, I will bring you a few more medallions for the collection. Martin wishes you the best, as do many of the gang you met during our trip to Athens.

As it is late, and I am being nudged by Dame Slumber to accept her embrace, I'll say goodnight. Just know your jumper misses and loves you more than ever.

Your boy,

Rayme

WHITE CITY STADIUM - London - July 20 - 2:30 pm

Even though the weather was less than desirable, Ray and Martin Sheridan were impressed with the number of spectators as they entered the White City stadium. They were escorted to the area around the broad jump pit, dropped their bags, and began their stretching exercises.

When Ray had finished stretching and was about to stand up, a hand reached down to help him. Ray looked up and saw a smiling fellow athlete with the Greek team emblem on his tunic.

Ray took his hand and when he stood up, he introduced himself. The athlete nodded and said in a thick Greek accent that he was Konstantine Tsiklitiras, pointed to the broad jump pit, and patted his chest as he spoke words in his native language. Ray had no way of understanding his words but knew what his gestures meant.

Martin informed Ray that Konstantine was the best jumper Greece had sent to the Games and he cautioned that this smiling Greek could possibly outjump them.

As Ray stood by the manicured broad jump landing pit, he counted twenty competitors for the event. The heats were set as in previous Olympics; three jumps for each athlete in the first round with the best eight jumpers moving on to compete in the final round of three jumps to determine the top three distances and then on to the medals round.

The dampness in the air and the occasional sprinkle of cold rain limited a sell-out audience in the stadium and gave the athletes cause for concern as the take-off bar, buried even with the grass, had to periodically be dried off.

As was his custom, Ray went into his crouch, and, for the first time, he heard a smattering of boos from the stands. Although somewhat disconcerted, once he went into his routine all sound was blocked out.

After the first round of jumps, every athlete complained to the British judges and officials about the sodden sand in the landing pit.

As each competitor climbed out of the pit they noticed their shoes were caked with heavy, wet sand. By the time the third round was complete, their shoes were soaked. The officials refused requests for additional dry sand to cover the puddles of rainwater pooling in the landing pit.

The result of the standing broad jump that day had Martin Sheridan a whisker-close third, with a jump of 10.7 feet to Tsiklitiras' second-place jump of 10.7 & ¼ feet. As Ray lifted off the bar, he knew his attempt would not equal his best from the St. Louis Games. He would have liked to have bettered his 1904 jump of 11.4 & 7/8 feet but finished with 10.11 & ¼ feet for the gold medal.

Letter to Nelle – July 21, 1908

Dearest Nelle,

Your boy came through yesterday with a first for the broad jump. I must admit that the conditions were unfavorable for an attempt to beat my St. Louis distance and, contrary to the majority of spectators, I am happy with the outcome.

Martin came in a close third behind a swell jumper from Greece who looks to be a formidable competitor in the future. I must confide in my girl the fact that Mother Nature seems to be withdrawing her favor for these weary muscles and bones.

The ever-present dampness here has caused some concern, as the time it takes to loosen the tight muscles and joints seems to take much longer than ever before.

I must also admit that in all honesty, the omission of the standing triple jump is a relief, as getting through the exhausting six jumps would take so much out of me that I would be fearful of a first in the high jump on the 23rd. Just two more rounds of high jumps to go, my darling girl, and then the return trip home to your loving arms, and my journey will be complete.

Be well and know I love you.

Your boy,

Rayme

38

BRIGHTON – The Boar and Thistle Pub - 1908

A wonderful memory disclosed in Ray's last Olympic journal from 1908 gave a different view of how the American athletes got along during their time with British counterparts while away from Olympic competition.

In a show of international sportsmanship, a large group of British athletes had driven their motorcars south to Brighton and invited some of the American track and field athletes to dine at a popular beachfront pub.

During the meal, many pints of warm ale were consumed amid the spirited and friendly discourse by all that attended. Many of the Brits were intrigued by Ray and his unbeaten record of jumps and soon both sides brought forth challenges.

Wagers were introduced as the Brits challenged the Americans to some informal contests on the beach in front of the pub. Cannonballs were used in the shot-put contest; a long broomstick held by two men was used as the high bar and later placed atop the pebbles on the beach to be the takeoff mark for the broad jump.

The Brits referred to Ray, being the oldest athlete in the bunch, as the "unbeatable old Yank", and once he had outdistanced all challengers, a very drunk athlete from Liverpool wagered that he could at least outjump Ray from a backward position from the mark.

"I'll pay for all the Yank's batch of expenses at the pub if I lose," he boasted.

At first, Ray politely refused the challenge, but due to the vocal urging of his fellow teammates and jeers from the Brits, he accepted and approached the broomstick.

The boastful Brit was first to jump. He stood behind the broomstick and began to swing his arms back and forth.

With a noisy exhale of air, he lifted backward in the air and although he made a valiant effort, he landed hard on his "bum".

A hat was placed where he landed as a chant swelled up from the corps of Brits, *"Yanks will fall...Yanks will fall!"*

Ray wrote that he knew his normal technique would be of no service to him jumping backward, so he simply went down into a crouch and fired upward, arching his back and throwing his legs up and over his body in a reverse summersault.

When his feet landed on the beach, the Americans roared their approval as it was evident that Ray had almost doubled the Brits' distance. The Brits cried "foul" at Ray's technique, but the loser kept his word and paid for the American's pub tab.

WHITE CITY STADIUM - July 23 - 1908

The periodic inclement weather had taken its toll on Ray's joints, aggravating his arthritis enough so that he needed more than just stretching to be ready for the final rounds of the standing high jump. During the train ride up to London, one of the trainers for the American team would sit on a stool at Ray's feet massaging his knee joints and leg muscles until they arrived.

As he did before each event, Ray went to the landing pit of the high jump venue and examined the condition of the grass on the take-off side and the landing pit. He stepped onto the marked take-off area and his shoes sank into the wet grass. A British official was passing by and Ray asked him if it had rained the night before and was told the night had passed dry and windy.

After Ray told him of his concerns about the overly sodden grass, Martin went to the high jump area and stepped onto the grass, and found it to be almost impossible to get a solid foundation to jump effectively. He was outraged and indicated that this was a case of deliberate sabotage.

His loud complaints caught the attention of a group of British officials who inspected the venue. They immediately postponed the event. A few minutes later the entire lineup of competitors was pleased to see that the officials had removed some bunting from a nearby tent and laid it over the area to absorb the excess water.

The incident had caused the standing high jump event to be backed up by more than an hour. The spectators in the stands began to hoot and whistle their disdain. The din of discontent grew ever louder as the first round of jumps commenced.

When the best hope for a British medal, Walter Henderson, failed to qualify, the crowd noise increased.

Since Ray knew there would be a rather long delay before the final jump, he and some of the Americans moved across the infield to observe the finish of the 400-meter race.

Three of their teammates, Will Robbins, Johnny Taylor and John Carpenter had all finished first in their individual qualifying rounds. Each had great expectations of besting the British champion, Wyndham Halswelle, who had taken second place in the 400-meter and third place in the 800-meter in the 1906 Athens Olympics.

As the Americans were approaching the inner edge of the track, the starter's pistol signaled the start of the race, so they watched the runners moving away from them toward the first of two turns of the oval.

Ray watched the tightly bunched runners make their way around the second set of curves until they began to jostle for the best position for the final stretch run to the finish line. Carpenter and Halswelle moved out in front, with Halswelle just off Carpenter's right shoulder.

According to many observers, this is the point when Carpenter, sensing Halswelle's presence, allegedly began to drift out into the center, forcing Halswelle to slow down and move toward the outside perimeter of the track.

Seeing this, the final turn official began running behind the runners waving his arms and wildly yelling for the line officials to cut the tape and declare the race unofficial. Halswelle heard the official and slowed to a gait, but Carpenter kept running full out and crossed the finish line beating Harry Hillman's 1906 time of 49.2 with the finishing time of 48.4 seconds.

The angry cries of the British spectators were deafening as Ray and the rest of his group walked back across the infield to the high jump venue. When they arrived at the apparatus, they saw that the bunting had absorbed the puddles and somehow new sod had been laid on the take-off side. The officials told all the competitors to prepare for the medal round of jumps.

The noise from the angry partisan spectators had diminished some, but not enough in the opinions of the competitors.

Many complained to the British judges and stated they would not jump unless the noise was curtailed.

When Ray was told his turn to jump would be after the two competitors standing near the bar, he went into his crouch and felt tightness in his knees.

He blocked out the crowd noise with his fingertips and began to envision the jump. Suddenly, the thought that this just might be the last jump of his Olympic career invaded his concentration. He fought off the demons of fatigue and pain and stood, ready for the jump.

As he approached the bar, the noise from the spectators began to swell to the point that no one could hear anyone else and the atmosphere became negatively electric.

Ray thought that going into his pre-jump arm swings would indicate to the crowd that he was about to jump and they would respectfully quiet down, but as those long slender arms began to swing back and forth, the noise level grew even louder.

He stopped his motion, stood up, looked at the stands and then at the officials to see if anything would be done with the vitriolic screams from the over sixty thousand spectators. They simply stared back at him and ordered him to continue.

Ray began the arm swing again and went into the final pre-jump crouch, but the deafening noise would not allow him to concentrate and he stood again. This time the same announcer rushed to the track and bellowed his commands through his megaphone at the crowd to cease the ruckus. Finally, when he warned them that the British entry would be penalized, the noise diminished quickly.

Ray was about to step onto the take-off bar for his final jump when Martin came over to him and shook his hand. He looked into Ray's eyes, smiled, and said, "Forget about them, old man. Just do what you do best!"

Ray knew that his fellow American, John Biller and the Greek jumper, Tsiklitiras had tied with leaps of 5 feet 1 inch.

He knew what he had to do, but for the first time, the condition of his legs introduced insecurity into his thoughts.

He settled into his routine, but this time he took twice as long with his arm swings and breathing. Finally, he fired off the newly installed sod.

His lead leg cleared the bar easily, but his trailing right leg felt heavy and his heart sank when he felt the heel of his jumping shoe touch the bar.

He landed awkwardly, and as he straightened up he expected the bar to fall to the ground next to him, but it stayed on the pegs, wobbling up and down.

The only cheers in the stadium came from the American spectators and the entire U.S. team as it became clear that Ray had cleared the bar at the gold medal height of 5 feet 2 inches.

He was immediately swarmed by his teammates who shouted their joy over his historic performance. After the adulation subsided, Tsiklitiras came over to Ray, shook his hand, and told him in broken English that he was the best in the world!

Ray had done what most thought impossible. He had successfully finished first in each event he had entered since that summer day at the 1900 Olympics in Paris, garnering the amazing total of ten individual gold medals. Ray was amused when some of his teammates reminded him that at the age of thirty-five, he was twice as old as some of the international athletes in the stadium.

The Swedish artist named Torsten Schonberg had been sitting in the stands across from the jumping apparatus watching intently as she sketched Ray during his rounds of the standing high jump. I found the drawing while researching the 1908 Olympics and to my utter delight, I discovered Miss Rebecca Jenkins, the author of a richly detailed book entitled, *"The First London Olympics - 1908"*.

I had the good fortune to be able to contact her and share thoughts about the 1908 Games.

On this occasion, she informed me she was in possession of Schonberg's original drawing.[18]

I was very pleased when she said yes to my request for using the drawing for the cover for "UNSUNG". I wish to thank Ms. Jenkins for this honor and her hard work and dedication to detail when writing her book on the London Games.

Her book is a "must read" for anyone interested in knowing the "real" story of the 1908 Olympics.

When the jumping events had concluded, the athletes were anxious to leave the White City stadium and board the train back to Brighton, but "Matty" Halpin urged them to wait in the infield until the more than 30,000 angry partisan British spectators had left the stands.

While waiting, Ray was approached by a reporter from the *New York Times* and asked his opinion of the 400-meter race. His response was published in the paper on July 21, 1908.

"At no time was there any lapping or confusion of the tracks. I thought Halswelle lost his head. He had the option of going either on the inside or the outside of Carpenter, but apparently, he could not make up his mind what to do."

Ray Ewry

---

[18] Ms. Rebecca Jenkins has given me permission to use the Schonberg drawing.

Ray based his response on the impressions of the runner's footfalls on the wet track and felt that Halswelle had options, but instead he slowed down and let the British track official run past him as he attempted to stop the race.

James Sullivan was outraged when the race was declared null and void and when the British official verdict came down that a new race was to be run, the American sprinters refused to partake.

Without any true competition from the U.S. sprinters, Halswelle easily won the second 400-meter race of the day. The 400-meter race wasn't the only event that outraged the volatile Mr. Sullivan.

He submitted complaints to the IOC and the BOC regarding the "tug-o-war" in which he claimed the British team of "bobbies" wore illegal, heavy work boots for the event, but the charges were ignored.

He did make progress after the Italian, Dorando Pietri, was illegally declared the winner of the marathon.

As Pietri was closing in on the finish line, his legs became wobbly and he began stumbling down the track. Just as he looked as though he would collapse, some British track officials ran to him and physically helped him cross the finish line.

The panel of international judges declared it was inappropriate for the officials to physically assist him. After long consideration, Johnny Hayes, the American long-distance runner who finished in second place, was declared the first-place winner.

The "all British" judging crew had proved to be so unfairly biased that Mr. Sullivan's protests were instrumental in changing the rules and regulations to ensure fair judging by an internationally appointed committee for all future Olympic Games.

During the closing ceremonies in the early afternoon of July 28th, the Duchess of Rutland and the Duchess of Westminster presented the silver and bronze medals respectively.

The athletes who finished out of the medals received their diplomas of merit and commemorative medals from Lady Desborough. King Edward was supposed to attend the awards and final closing ceremonies but declined due to his resentment of "bad press" and overall negative opinions from those damned "Yanks".

He wanted nothing to do with the Olympics since he felt the integrity of the British officials had been denigrated and England's image tarnished.

In his stead, Queen Alexandra was chosen to award the gold medals and it was noted that all the American champions politely bowed before the Queen as they received their medals.

And so, after the awards ceremony ended, the London Olympics, comprised of 22 nations, 110 events, and 2,008 athletes, came to a close.

The memories the athletes and officials carried home were both joyous and bitter, but overall the Games were a turning point in the legacy of the Olympics, with the various international committees vowing to correct any faults and make each ensuing Olympics better than the previous one.

Ray's experiences in the 1908 Olympic Games were the last entries recorded in his final journal. Relying on other authors' and researchers' publications for minor anecdotes on Ray, I ran across another interesting topic while I was reading the fabulous book written by Fred G. Jarvis, *"From Vision to Victory"*.

In his chapter dedicated to the 1912 Stockholm Olympics, he writes that Ray, while trying to qualify for the Games in New York, had attempted to clear the high bar, not in his championship form as he had done in the 1908 London Games, but as a running high jumper.

Mr. Jarvis states that Ray attempted the trial running high jump and had an unfortunate landing that ruptured a kidney. This attempt and its result sounded the "death knell" for Ray's hope to compete in his fifth Olympics.

I am attempting to learn more about this and will update my records if I find more information about his injury.

40

BALTIMORE – 1982

One morning my phone rang five times before I could answer and the voice on the phone sounded aggravated.

"Hello!" I mumbled.

"Good morning! I am trying to reach Mr. Thomas Carson," stated the caller in a very formal manner. Something in the voice was faintly familiar.

"May I ask who's calling?"

"This is Paul Harvey from Chicago."

"Paul Harvey...from that radio show?"

"One and the same! Are you Mr. Carson?"

It really was Paul Harvey and I had to ask myself the obvious question, *"Now what would the famous Paul Harvey want with me?"*

"Yes...yes. I'm sorry to sound so vague. I just woke up."

"Quite understandable, young man. Do you have time for a few questions?" he asked.

"Of course, Mr. Harvey...ask away."

Mr. Harvey informed me that he was going to do a segment on Ray for his syndicated radio program, *"The Rest of the Story"*. He said that while researching, he came across a few historical anomalies and he wanted to go right to the horse's mouth, so to speak, to get the correct information.

He asked for Ray's birth date, his years at Purdue, and finally what was my relationship to him. I answered all his questions and was disappointed that he didn't have more time for me to elaborate on my new findings with the journals.

He told me the approximate date of the broadcast and as quickly as the call came in, it ended. Now, I felt like things were starting to happen.

I have the original recording taken from the radio/cassette deck during a nasty thunderstorm on the day of the broadcast.

There's quite a lot of static due to the lightning strikes, but there's no mistaking that wonderful, iconic voice of Paul Harvey.

The following is **Paul Harvey's** actual 1980 radio transcript from

"The Rest of the Story".

"They called him Ewry…a young lad growing up, apparently normally, in Lafayette, Indiana. The backyard of his home was near the Wabash Canal…wonderful place for a youngster to run and play."

"Then, one afternoon Ray's play hours were cut short by a headache and sore throat. His mother felt her son's forehead and it was hot.

"Off to bed, young man!"

"At first, young Ray did not appreciate the confinement, but after a while, he was too sick to care. He got a tummy ache and then his neck and his back started hurting."

"That'll teach you to go out without your jacket young man!"

"Ray agreed, and after a few days, he was well enough to return to his backyard play. Now I wish we could end the story right here, but we cannot. You see…within a few more days young Ray was overcome by a strange weakness. By inches, his legs seemed to be turning to lead."

"Growing frightened, he told his mother. His mother called the doctor and after a thorough examination the physician, stood there shaking his head."

"Perhaps another doctor should be consulted," he said, but he knew what it was, and Ray's mother knew that he knew, and scared inside, she demanded the truth and was told…Poliomyelitis. Her son had polio."

"At best," the doctor said, "Ray would become an invalid, would be confined to a wheelchair for the rest of his life. And yet, the attack had been so severe that it was doubtful young Ray would even survive. In a moment…the rest of the story."

{Commercial break}

"Ray Ewry was only a boy when polio presented him with the options of death or life in a wheelchair, and as the doctors summoned by his anxious parents paraded past his bedside, each confirmed the diagnosis and the prognosis. At best, Ray would soon be entirely…permanently unable to walk."

"Then, at the end of this long procession of physicians came one doctor with a possible prescription… jumping.

Jumping? Jumping, though the other doctors said it would not do any good, but it wouldn't hurt to try. That young Ray should get out of bed and get into that nice big backyard of his and start jumping over anything."

"Jumping! Jumping barrels, bushes, bushel baskets. To this day, nobody remembers the doctor's name, and nobody knows why on earth he offered such an experimental "homespun" prescription for such a dread disease."

"And yet, I suppose in retrospect, we can say that the exercise was not too unlike that which Sister Kenny subsequently proved effective. But anyway, this we know!"

"Young Ray mustered all the energy…all of the courage that he could manage, and he gave the prescription a try and he did not stop jumping until he made the highest jump of all; an astounding, bounding leap into the record books."

They said he would be unable to walk. Instead, he learned to run. For Raymond Clarence Ewry…E.W.R.Y… in case you want to look it up, eventually won ten individual Olympic gold medals in track. That's right! That makes Ray the winningest Olympic athlete of all time."

(Pause)

"And now you know the rest of the story."

NEW YORK CITY - August 6 - 1908

Many of the American athletes returned home on the White Star steamship, *"Adriatic"*, to a throng of adoring celebrants. Nelle was overjoyed as Ray and the other athletes came down the ramp amid the cacophony of cheers and brass band music.

A *New York Times* reporter interviewed Ray about the 26.2-mile Marathon in London. The following quote was published the next day.

"The officers and at times spectators were most unfair, and they lost no opportunity of rubbing it into us all they could. The pulling of the Italian over the finish line in the Marathon race was an outrageous piece of work. This is shown in the moving pictures of the race that were taken."

"I believe if those who had been following this runner around the course had seen that it was a runner from Great Britain who was in second place they would have been willing to hit Dorando over the head rather than have him cross the line. But it was an American who was in second place, so they wanted the Italian to win."

On August 29th, the U.S. Olympic Team was honored with a splendid parade from Broadway and 46th Street to City Hall. It was reported that colorful marching bands, followed by over 15,000 members of the various military branches, led the parade before 250,000 people. Next in line came the floats carrying the 95 Olympic athletes, team officials, managers, and coaches.

The city's Irish spectators cheered wildly as the float carrying James E. Sullivan, the marathon winner Johnny Hayes, and the American and Irish flags passed by.

Prominently displayed on the stage among the colorful banners of the many local athletic clubs was the American flag that Ralph Rose refused to dip before the King and Queen of England during the closing ceremonies.

President Theodore Roosevelt could not attend the parade or the following presentation of commemorative medals to the athletes but tendered an open invitation for the team and staff to join him at his summer home at Oyster Bay, New York for a private celebration later in the week.

OYSTER BAY – Sagamore Hill – August 31, 1908

Two days later, James E. Sullivan, "Matty" Halpin, Mike Murphy, and the rest of the Olympic Athletes boarded a motor launch and sailed from

New York City harbor to the waters just off Sagamore Hill.

The tide was out and the water too low to carry the athletes to the private dock, so the launch was moored offshore and the passengers were ferried by an armada of private rowboats.

Once on shore, Mr. Sullivan had the athletes form two rows and the entire group marched up the hill to the President's summer home while whistling, *"There'll Be A Hot Time In The Old Town Tonight"*.

The Olympians paraded before the President and Mrs. Roosevelt and when they had grouped before the President, he praised them for their gallant participation in the Olympics and the national pride that they engendered from all the citizens of America.

"I think it is the literal truth, Mr. Sullivan, to say that the feat that this team has performed has never been duplicated in the history of athletics. I think it is the biggest feat that has ever been performed by any team of any nation, and I congratulate all of you."

President Theodore Roosevelt

Part of Ray's speech was delivered during a banquet held by the A.A.U. in New York after the President's Oyster Bay affair.

"To have been with my teammates who persevered through the dismal weather and questionable fairness of the judging in London and standing before the President as he extolled praise on our efforts, was simply an unparalleled experience in my lifetime."

BALTIMORE - 1994

During the summer months of 1994, I began a long-distance relationship with the venerable Mrs. Alameda McCullough, the elderly curator of the Tippecanoe County Historical Society. During one phone conversation about Ray's past, she said that I should contact someone at the local newspaper, the *Lafayette Journal & Courier.*

The next day, I phoned their offices and was transferred to the news department. I was introduced and subsequently interviewed by Paula Waltz and John Norberg, who wrote very nice articles about my project. In both articles, they mentioned that I was in the beginning stages of writing a book to bring Ray's forgotten legacy into public view.

A week after the articles were published, I received a letter from Dr. Cindy Eberts, Ph.D., the wife of a young professor at Purdue University. She stated that she too had been researching Ray's accomplishments in hopes of writing a book on his life. She had a writer friend who had transplanted from Los Angeles and wanted to collaborate with her on the project.

Cindy disclosed that she had done some in-depth research on Ray and offered to help me understand the chronological events that occurred in Lafayette, Indiana in the 1890s.

It was frustrating to be so far from the proverbial "ground zero" of my research and I needed to get out to Lafayette to be surrounded by Ray's environment, but obligations prohibited me from doing so at that time.

One morning in early September, Dame Fortune chose to visit me in the form of a phone call from a man named Thomas V. Carson.

I had never met much less spoken to him, but over the years I had heard from a few mutual acquaintances about the hassles the similarity of our names had caused this gentleman.

He introduced himself and I instantly began to apologize for causing him so much grief over the years. He explained to her that there was another Baltimorean named Thomas Carson living just a few miles away who was an entertainer and the calls had to be for him.

After we cleared up that part of our pasts, he informed me that the reason for his call was to give me the name and phone number of a representative from Purdue University who had been searching for the grandson of Ray Ewry.

I called the number and reached Mr. Jim Vruggink, who worked in the Athletic Department with the Athletic Director, Morgan Burke. He informed me that Ray was to be inducted into the inaugural class of the Purdue Sports Hall of Fame and the school was requesting me to represent him posthumously.

Of course, I agreed, and he said he would have his secretary send me all the appropriate invitations and clearances for the events that would take place in a few weeks.

When the formal invitation came, I was thrilled. I was especially excited to see the name Chris Shenkel as the Master of Ceremonies.

It was then that I knew this was going to be very special. Then I read the names of the other honorees and was floored.

John Wooden, Bob Griese, Terry Dischinger and Leroy Keyes were some highly respected names in the present world of sports in America.

PURDUE UNIVERSITY - 1994 - Sports Hall of Fame Induction

When I arrived in Indianapolis for the one-night banquet and induction ceremony, I marveled at the way the architects and builders had transformed an old train station into a fancy Holiday Inn.

Due to Ray's notoriety, I was set to do two radio interviews before leaving for the Indiana Roof Ballroom. Time was tight, but we got them done.

At the banquet, the Hall of Fame inductees were escorted on stage and seated at tables on either side of the speaker's podium. Before each inductee was invited to speak, a short audio/video presentation splashed on a giant screen behind us.

After Ray's historical montage, I was introduced as his grandson. Gathering myself, I thanked the staff at Purdue and the people of Lafayette for this honor and went on to describe how my mother had planted the seed for my project. It seemed to take forever, but the speech lasted only five or so minutes.

As I turned to shake Jim Vruggink's hand, I saw Ray's giant photo up on the screen and got a lump in my throat. Then, Mr. Vruggink handed me a plaque with Ray's picture and his records on it and the audience went wild.

I stood there holding this object of appreciation from a grateful group of sports enthusiasts and I raised it high over my head like it was the Super Bowl Trophy or the Stanley Cup.

The thundering applause for Ray was a very special experience for me. It was as if these people recognized what Ray had suffered through as a child with polio and how he had changed his life.

The next morning, I drove to West Lafayette to meet the induction committee at Morgan Burke's house for a social cocktail party before the "Little Brown Jug" football game.

It was the day of the massive rivalry between Purdue and the University of Indiana.

It was refreshing to meet so many people who knew of Ray since no one I knew in Baltimore had ever heard of him other than Jim McKay and the gang at WJZ-TV.

All the inductees and their families were hustled outside and taken to a staging area where we were ushered onto the famous "Boilermaker" train to be driven across campus to Ross-Aide stadium.

As we entered the parking lot of the stadium on that beautiful November afternoon, I saw more than ten thousand "tailgaters" in both the Purdue black and gold and the I.U. red and white colors.

There were hundreds of flags and banners waving in the autumn breeze as the aroma created by the thousands of grills cooking burgers, hot dogs, chicken, brats, ribs, and any kind of concoction known to man, wafted through the smoky air. It was electric.

The inductees were seated in the front row at the fifty-yard line and when the second quarter ended, we were ushered onto the field and told to wait in the center.

At the far end of the field, a monstrous jumbotron began to portray the same audio/video presentation of the inductees as we had seen during the induction ceremony in Indianapolis the night before.

As each inductee was introduced, Jim Vruggink walked over and shook our hands. The crowd noise was deafening, and it was at that moment that I realized Ray had stood in this exact stadium during its grand opening dedication exactly seventy years before.

The next day, I went to the Eberts' home for lunch. The Eberts were very cordial and Holly was quite unique, disclosing she had written for Disney a few years before. I was getting more and more excited as all three of us began the initial phase of our collaboration.

I had brought a variety of Ray's memorabilia and displayed it on their dining room table after the meal and was pleased to see how excited they were to see items that only a blood relative would have had.

I left there feeling like this was going to be a great union of minds. Around nine o'clock that night, Cindy called me and said she had some very important news she had just discovered. This one phone call helped me solve one of the most important mysteries surrounding Ray's post-Olympic legacy: the final resting place of Ray and Nelle Ewry, but more on this later.

44

DOUGLAS MANOR - 1912

During the four years following the 1908 Olympics, Ray continued his dominance in A.A.U. competitions. At the national indoor championships held at Madison Square Garden in 1909, Ray won two more gold medals. He was also invited to display his championship jumping form at many public and charitable expositions around the New York area, but his distances began to diminish due to the increasing presence of his old demons; rheumatic fever and arthritis.

Ray's new job as Chief Engineer for the New York Board of Water Supply made it possible for the Ewry's to leave Bayonne and purchase a beautiful small estate called Douglas Manor in Douglaston, Long Island. Now he had enough space in the backyard to erect the state-of-the-art high-jump apparatus presented to him by Mr. A. G. the year before.

In 1911, while training for the upcoming Stockholm Olympics, he confided in Nelle that his body just wasn't performing as it used to, but his dogged determination to overcome his shortcomings compelled him to push himself harder. It never crossed his mind that he wouldn't be in proper form to compete in the 1912 Games.

On an early spring day in 1912, his old pal Martin Sheridan, hearing of Ray's diminishing distances, came out to Douglas Manor. Nelle met him at the front door and asked him to come to the rear dining room and look out onto the spacious backyard where Ray was practicing the standing high jump.

The man who took the bronze medal in the two standing jumps at the 1906 Athens Olympics watched as his best friend tried and failed to make it over the high bar numerous times.

Martin and Nelle winced each time Ray attempted a jump as it became obvious that every landing caused Ray pain, but both knew that never stopped him before.

Frustrated, Ray finally finished his drills and came back to the house to see Martin and enjoy a quiet lunch.

Ray recorded in his last journal that during this lunch, after Nelle had excused herself, Martin commented on how hard Ray's training had become and suggested that at age 38, it just might be time for Ray to hang it up.

If he was selected to be on the 1912 Olympic team, he would be competing against athletes close to half his age and with the newer techniques in training, twice his strength. Martin talked about the younger, stronger U.S. athletes waiting in the wings to compete and wouldn't it be best to go out on top as the greatest jumper in Olympic history.

After all, Ray was undefeated in the ten events he had entered in four straight Olympics and his accomplishments were in the history books. Ray took Martin's comments to heart and after a few moments of contemplation, he agreed. It was time.

He realized his responsibilities at the New York Department of Water Supply were demanding more of his time away from home and it was painfully obvious he couldn't continue jumping at world-class levels. His time as an Olympian was over.

Ray stood and slowly walked across the backyard to the high jump apparatus. He bent over, picked up the bar, gently placed it on the pegs, and almost in reverence, ran his hand slowly along the length.

He squatted down, dropped a hand, and raked his fingers in the dirt. He scooped up a handful and let it filter through his fingers, then turned and walked away from the landing pit for the last time.

There would be no more rushing to the practice fields or the training rooms at the NYAC; no more challenging the bar on the high-jump apparatus or landing in the long dirt and cinder pits of the broad and triple jumps, and no more "Human Frog" or "Rubberman" references in newspapers.

In 1912, at the age of 39, Raymond Clarence Ewry, holder of world records in countless collegiate competitions, A.A.U., and athletic club championships, and having achieved the unprecedented record of winning ten individual Olympic gold medals, reluctantly retired from Olympic competition. It was the end of an era of perfection and domination of the standing jumps.

For many years after this retirement, Ray was enlisted to judge hundreds of track & field events throughout the Mid-Atlantic States.

MARY ELIZABETH EWRY

On the 27th of April 1919, at age 39, Nelle Johnson Ewry gave birth to a healthy, seven-and-a-half-pound girl at the Sloane Hospital for Women at 447 W. 59th Street in New York City. She was named Mary Elizabeth Ewry.

She was destined to grow up in a loving home with adoring parents who, instead of the traditional Mary or Lizzie, Ray and Nelle decided to call her Betsy.

45

PURDUE UNIVERSITY – Ross-Aide Stadium - 1924

The weekend of "homecoming" was always a special event in Lafayette. The organizers from Purdue had booked numerous alumni to address the students, faculty, and fellow alumnae. Ray was scheduled to make his short speech and presentation at halftime.

As the teams trotted off the field after the first half, Ray was escorted to the end zone where the track and field apparatus was set. A microphone stand had been placed next to the broad jump landing pit and Ray was placed nearby. A gentleman in top hat and tails approached the microphone and tapped on it.

For the introduction, he spoke of Ray's Purdue years and continued with his A.A.U., New York Athletic Club, and Olympic accomplishments. The audience's standing ovation roared across the field as Ray approached the microphone, cradling the Grecian urn. The ovation lasted for over two minutes and ceased only after Ray extended a long arm into the air.

The following speech was hand-written on a piece of Purdue stationary I found in Betsy Ewry's archives.

"Thank you for the honor of being chosen to speak here today and for this fine welcome. I want to thank the organizers for asking me to be a part of this special dedication of the new Ross-Ade stadium."

"In my travels as a member of the Purdue track and field team, a member of the New York Athletic Club, and later as a member of the United States Olympic team, I competed on athletic fields from Indiana to the Pre-Catalan in Paris, Francis Field in St. Louis to the stadiums in Athens and London."

"I carried the true spirit and love of competition that I learned here at Purdue. Trying to be the best that one can be was the only way of showing my thanks and respect for this great institution of learning until one day, while at the Athens Olympics of 1906, I thought of an idea that might mean something to the future athletes."

"Today, I bring to Ross-Ade stadium, and to the men and women who will compete here, hallowed soil from the ancient Olympic stadium in Athens, Greece. This soil represents the place where combatants gathered, not on the battlefield, but on the peaceful grounds of the Olympic stadium to compete for the glory of their country."

"Again, I thank you for this honor and I hope that future athletes who will perform here will honor the athletes who competed on this soil by carrying on the grand tradition of the sport by being the best they can be and to remember always, Citius, Altius, Fortius! Go Boilermakers!"

46

DOUGLAS MANOR - LONG ISLAND - 1930

Back in New York, the years flew by. Due to new challenges from the burgeoning population growth in New York State, Ray was placed in charge of numerous projects for the New York Board of Water Supply, primarily dealing with building dams and conduits for water transport to New York City.

At home, 11-year-old Betsy enjoyed a happy childhood with her father teaching her the glory of sports and the meaning of "loyalty to team", while her mother taught her fairness and compassion.

There was always a peaceful battle between Ray and Nelle as to how Betsy would be raised. Ray was thrilled that his daughter could swim faster than the boys she knew and out-shoot any of them with the bow and arrow. She was his "tomboy" beauty.

Nelle on the other hand, wanted Betsy to be schooled in the feminine arts and enrolled her in music and art classes, and taught her to cook and care for the house and grounds.

When Betsy was old enough, Nelle enrolled her in the Girl Scouts. It was this one action that allowed Betsy to establish her independence, confidence, and the desire to help others.

Tragedy struck idyllic Douglas Manor when Nelle became seriously ill, and after a long vigil, she finally passed from tuberculosis in 1931.

Ray and Betsy were devastated, but both made promises to Nelle they would honor her request for them to be strong and to carry on in her memory. Betsy kept her promise to her mother by excelling in high school while Ray continued his involvement as a line judge for athletic events and guided Betsy in the right direction.

She finished in the top ten of her senior class and was offered a full scholarship to the prestigious Maryland College for Women in Lutherville, Maryland, a suburb of Baltimore.

Thrilled to be going to college as an independent woman, but with a heavy heart, Betsy Ewry took the train to Baltimore and enrolled at the college. Less than a month after she arrived in Lutherville, the most devastating news of her life was delivered by telegram.

NEW YORK TIMES OBITUARY COLUMN
THURSDAY, SEPTEMBER 30, 1937

RAY C. EWRY, STAR
OF OLYMPIC TEAMS

Winner of More Titles Than
Any Other Athlete Dies At
Home in Douglas Manor

Ray C. Ewry, maker of world's records a generation ago in the standing high and standing broad jumps, who won more Olympic championships than any other athlete in the world, American or foreign, died last night at his home 343 Ridge Road, Douglas Manor, Queens, after a three month illness. On October 14, he would have been 63 years old.

In the track and field events of the Olympics Games at Paris in 1900, St. Louis in 1904, Athens in 1906, and London in 1908, Mr. Ewry won first place in both the standing high and broad jumps, and in 1900 in Paris, and 1904 in St. Louis, he also captured the standing hop, step and jump. His world's record for the standing broad jump, 11 feet 4 7/8 inches, established at St. Louis had never been equalled.

Mr. Ewry was born at Lafayette Ind., a son of the late George and Elizabeth Ewry. He was a graduate of Purdue University, holding the degree of civil engineer. After the Olympics of 1908 he retired from competition, but remained a familiar figure at track meets in the East and often served as an official for jumping contests. For many years, including the period of his track triumphs, he had been a member of the New York Athletic Club.

In his volume, " The Story of the Olympic Games ", John Kieran, describing the Paris meet of 1900, refers to July 16 " as the day that saw Ray Ewry, a tall, lanky fellow wearing the Winged Foot emblem of the New York A.C. begin his record run of Olympic victories. The remarkable thing about Ewry was that he was an invalid as a small boy. His life was despaired of, but the family physician suggested that he might build himself up by taking certain exercises. He improved his health and enlarged his experience to take in jumping. While a student at Purdue he began to excel as a jumper."

Although he was nearly 27 years old when he first appeared in Olympic competition, he was on four Olympic teams and won 10 Olympic championships.

Since 1912, Mr. Ewry had been with the New York Board of Water Supply, latterly as a supervising engineer on the Ashokan system.

His wife, Nell Johnson Ewry, also a native of Lafayette, Ind., and a graduate of Purdue, died in 1931. A daughter, Mary Elizabeth Ewry, survives. Funeral services will be held in the Community Church, Douglaston, at 8 o'clock this evening.

NEW YORK – 1937

On September 29, 1937, after overcoming the crippling effects of Polio, enduring life-long bouts of rheumatic fever, and dealing with painful arthritis in his later years, Ray lost the first competition of his life.

He had battled through a three-month illness and finally died at his home at Douglas Manor, leaving his only child to carry on the Ewry lineage as an 18-year old college freshman.

Stunned and afraid of the future, Betsy had to travel back to Long Island to take care of the arrangements.

When Ray passed on September 29, 1937, the *New York Times* obit column written the next day stated that he would be placed next to Nelle in the cemetery of the Community Church in Douglaston.

A few days after the funeral, she met with her father's executor of the Ewry estate and numerous legal representatives to arrange the dissolution of the estate and all other family matters.

On Thursday night, September 30, 1937, an audience of over two hundred people listened to dozens of eulogies given in Ray's honor.

After Betsy gave a heartfelt eulogy and said her final farewell to her father, a representative from President Franklin D. Roosevelt's office gave a moving eulogy wherein he extolled Ray's patriotism and spoke of his athletic accomplishments.

In closing, he presented Betsy with a commemorative civilian medal of honor with the following sentiment:

"Ms. Ewry, your father exemplified all that is Olympian and American."

On one of my numerous New York City visits, I went to the church in Douglaston and was shown the grid for the gravesite locations of Ray and Nelle Ewry. I drove down the tree-lined road to the designated section and searched in vain for over an hour.

No such graves were found, not even a headstone. I returned to the office and informed the attendant that I could not find any trace of the Ewry's.

Upon returning to the office, the attendant told me that their records were up to date and that I must have the spelling wrong.

I produced the obit column from the *New York Times,* but that did no good. He had no explanation as to why I couldn't locate the graves and remained adamant that they were out there. I tried to reason with him, but he dismissed me.

47

LUTHERVILLE, MARYLAND – 1941

During her college years, Betsy attended many track and field events in the Maryland area and met a track star for the University of Maryland, my dad, Thomas E. Carson, IV. They were married in 1941, and I was born on April 20th, 1943 while Dad was overseas flying in B-17s as a navigator during WW II.

Betsy became a teacher in the Baltimore school system and taught challenged children for many years. Unfortunately, my mother and father divorced in 1961, so Betsy decided to advance her education and received her Master's Degree in Psychology. She moved to Henderson, South Carolina to teach at Clemson University until Alzheimer's forced her to retire in 1978.

One of the hardest things I ever had to do was to place her in an assisted living environment. Being very strong physically, she spent many years in her own mental purgatory and finally passed on December 26, 1992.

I arranged a small memorial to be held at her favorite place of worship, the Church of the Redeemer in Baltimore, and to my surprise, over 500 people arrived to mourn her passing. The outpouring of love and respect showed to her in return for her many years of dedication and compassion overwhelmed me.

With her abundance of patience and compassion, Betsy was a strong influence on my sister Jan and me. Her basic joy and lust for life were filled with much more happiness than sadness and she always carried her head high as the daughter of an Olympic champion.

She taught us to never let adversity dim our dreams and to carry on no matter what life had to offer. It was obvious that Ray's will to overcome such a daunting thing as Polio was passed on to her and then on to us.

48

BALTIMORE - 1998

In August, a promoter invited me to be the closing speaker at an Olympic memorabilia collector's convention at the newly restored Savage Mill conference room just south of Columbia, Maryland. He wanted me to bring as much of my Ray Ewry memorabilia as I could for display.

When I arrived at Savage Mill, he told me he thought it would be an interesting twist to the night if I withheld who I was and ask the audience of collectors certain pointed questions about the early Olympics and what my relationship to them might be.

Standing before over thirty collectors from around the world, I began to unfold my story and asked anyone to raise their hand if they thought they knew how I was related to the Olympics.

Incorrect answers came at me for about ten minutes until I said the word "polio". At that point, a man in the back of the room fired his answer up to me in a booming voice...

"Ray Ewry! You must be a relative!"

Many of the collectors queried me as to the 10 Olympic gold medals. I had to tell them that the medals were stolen in 1978 and that little bit of information caused gasps in the audience. It made me feel good that they felt the theft was a travesty. It was at that point that I felt I had their rapt attention, so I began to tell them another story about the theft that had a positive outcome.

I told them about one morning in 1984, as I was getting out of the shower when the phone rang. It was a call from the Chicago national headquarters of the Amateur Athletic Union. The caller, a polite female, placed me on hold, so I sat there dripping wet.

Finally, a young man came on line and again asked if I was a relative of Raymond C. Ewry and I affirmed that I was.

He said he had good news for me. I kept my impatience in check as he began to tell me an incredible story.

It seems a woman in Houston, Texas had just finished the last of the family shopping for the week. She paid for the groceries and was heading across the large parking lot when something from the ground caught her eye.

She told the A.A.U. spokesman that a glint, a golden reflection, caused her to look down. She leaned over and saw a gold coin near the rear tire of a car. When she picked it up, she couldn't quite make out what it was, so she spits on it, rubbed it against her jeans, and took a closer look.

At first, she was disappointed that it wasn't a silver dollar or a minted

coin of some high value. She was in a hurry to get back to her kids, so she put the coin in her jeans pocket and continued to her car.

Three days later, as she was loading her washing machine, the coin fell from her jeans. She retrieved it and went into her living room to get a magnifying glass she kept on her desk.

In her hand was a commemorative coin from the 1908 London Olympics.

In the top section of the identification border it read:

IV OLYMPIAD LONDON 1908

At the bottom of the border it read:

RAY EWRY USA

Inside the border was the profile of a man's head and I must say, once I saw it in person, it held a striking resemblance to Ray's facial features.

Superimposed on the head was the figure of a man jumping over a bar. Then she turned the coin over. On the flip side of the coin, the three Latin words that signify the Olympics crested the top half of a banner.

"CITIUS ALTIUS FORTIUS"

Below the banner were the five interlocking rings that have always represented the five continents. In the center was my grandfather's name:

"RAY EWRY"

In a much smaller font, the following words:

"Completes sweep of competition in standing jumping events"

The bottom of the coin portrayed the traditional olive sprigs presented to the winners in the ancient Olympics. They were clipped from the olive trees that grew in the Altis of the athletic shrine of Olympia in Elis.

Since the coin held no obvious value to her, she tried to think of what to do with it. She decided to go to the library and look up the name, Ray Ewry.

She was taken to the Olympic section and pulled down three books: "An Approved History of the Olympic Games" by Bill Henry, "The Olympic Games" by C. Robert Paul, and "The Story of the Olympic Games" by John Kiernan.

When she came to page 34 in Mr. Paul's book, there was a photograph of Ray Ewry jumping over the high bar.

It was the exact photo that the engraver used as a template for the image superimposed over Ray's head on the coin.

Why she didn't call the United States Olympic Committee is an unanswered question, but I am forever grateful that by calling the A.A.U. she enabled the only item from the stolen Ray Ewry collection to be returned to its rightful heirs.

After my short presentation, I uncovered Ray's memorabilia on two long tables. As the host ended the meeting, about half the audience came to my tables and fussed over the memorabilia they had never seen before.

I must admit I had to keep a watchful eye on these strangers, as most of them were the "touchy-feely" type and wanted to handle the trophies, medals, and odd items on display.

When the meeting was finally over and I was packing up my gear, I noticed a blank white card on the table with my name written in longhand.

I picked it up, thinking it must have been a place card or a nametag. I turned it over and read the few scribbled words on the card and felt my knees almost buckle.

"Info on medals...parking lot...black Volvo wagon"

I thanked my host and hustled out the door to the parking lot.

I locked my gear in my SUV before scanning the almost empty parking lot. I saw a few SUVs and a sedan close to the building and stepped away from my van to see a black Volvo wagon parked in a far corner of the darkened lot. I lit a cigarette and as casually as I could, walked toward the Volvo. My heart was racing with the hope of finding any information about Ray's stolen medals. It was the only thing I could focus on at that moment.

As I got to within twenty feet, I heard the engine start and as the Volvo suddenly charged past me, the driver tossed two cards from the window.

As I picked up the cards, I caught sight of the New York license plate. I stood there in the dark feeling as if I was in a B-grade mystery movie. I looked at what turned out to be a postcard with Ray's image on the front and a picture and actual signature on the back. It had the postmark Minneapolis from 1990.

What would cause this person to set me up like that? A practical joke, a tease...or maybe they really had some information on the medals and just got cold feet. Why did they drive off without talking with me? The mystery of the medals continues.

2008 - BEL AIR, MARYLAND

In the spring of 2008, I ventured into the Barnes & Noble bookstore in White Marsh, Maryland to find something to occupy my reading time. I found that at that moment none of the mystery, adventure, or historical books interested me.

I managed to end up in the "writer's section" and began to scan the shelves for something other than the redundant books about how to become a successful writer. Luckily, one title jumped out at me. It was the book by Thomas Monteleone entitled, *"The Complete Idiot's Guide to Writing a Novel"*.

It was on sale that day, so I bought it. To my delight, I found the writing to be light, a quick read, and not too preachy like many of the "how-to" books on writing have been. Tom had me laughing on several occasions, and once I finished the book, I realized we had a few things that were remarkably in common.

His favorite NFL football team is the Baltimore Ravens. He went to a private school with Jesuit instructors and he sold cable in the early 1980s.

I happened to work for a company that provides security for the Baltimore Ravens and at the time of the reading, I was working for Comcast Cablevision. The final coincidence was that I also went to a private school, St. Paul's School for Boys, whereas Tom went to Loyola.

In the back of the book, Tom had printed his e-mail address with a note that anyone interested in commenting on the book could write him...so I did.

It was, if I remember correctly, no more than a week before my cell phone rang. My Caller ID function displayed a 443 prefix, which I knew was a Maryland number. When I asked who was calling and the caller said Tom Monteleone, I could have been knocked down with a feather.

He explained that he had moved from his home in New England so his daughter could attend a highly regarded school in Baltimore to enhance her chances of gaining entrance to a good college.

He was living with his wife and daughter in a small town north of Baltimore in Harford County, 25 miles from me. He explained that he was a published author of award-winning horror and suspense novels and his wife had a publishing company called Borderlands Press. Then he asked me the question that brought my Ray Ewry project full circle.

"Tom, do you know a guy named Steve Yeager?"

"I sure do. He was a fraternity brother of mine many years ago, and he owns a small movie production company here. Why?"

"Because I've known Steve for many years too, and in 1981 he brought me an unfinished script he wanted me to look over."

"The script was called "UNSUNG" and it was about a courageous Olympic jumper named Ray Ewry."

"That was my very first attempt at writing!" I exclaimed. "I know it was just awful."

"Not so fast! It wasn't that bad."

I felt somewhat pleased that my rookie effort wasn't completely panned.

"I thought the storyline was a good one, but I never heard anything more about it."

Tom informed me about his Borderlands Boot Camp for new writers and after the three-day event, he urged me to write not only about Ray but combine Ray's story with my own struggles in researching and obtaining answers to my many questions about Ray's legacy and his mementos.

I owe Tom so much for pointing me in the right direction and giving me the insight to carry on. Once I transposed the project from my old script to primarily prose, it took off and my special appreciation goes out to my friend and writing mentor, Tom Monteleone.

49

BALTIMORE, MARYLAND - 2010

In September, I received the following e-mail from Mr. Jim Roberts from New York. With Mr. Roberts's permission, I felt it only proper to add his amazing disclosures to this body of work.

Greetings:

I am an engineer with the NYC Department of Environmental Protection. Recently a colleague, who knew of my appreciation for your grandfather's contribution to the enduring legacy of NYC's water supply system, forwarded a link from Purdue University's website that contained a profile of Ray Ewry. I was frankly flabbergasted.

Those of us who are the modern stewards of the greatest engineering feat in modern times, the NYC water supply system, often think of a man named J. Waldo Smith as the one most responsible for its development and success. I am responsible for many of the tunnel and dam assets that make up this system and I know what many do not.

In my research, I was fortunate to come upon a series of diary entries from one Ray Ewry. After years of study, I have come to respect your grandfather as perhaps one of the most unsung heroes in NYC history. Ubiquitous doesn't quite capture the breadth and scope of Ray Ewry's involvement in the design, inspection, and commissioning of the various pieces of our great system. Far more than once I have been involved in a conversation where I could explain something that nobody else even knew about.

When asked how I could know whatever the topic was I explain I have Ray Ewry's diary. Who knew he was such an outstanding athlete as well.

I guess successful and committed people are just that...successful! I have tremendous respect for Ray Ewry's contributions to our system. Wow! Good luck with your endeavor and be proud of your grandfather.

Sincerely,

Jim Roberts

Within a few days, I contacted Mr. Roberts and an informative relationship began. Over the last year and a half, he has passed on a great deal of data about Ray Ewry's contributions to the daunting task that was the planning and construction of various dams and aqueducts in the Catskills that supply New York City with water in the early years of the 20th century.

I was interested in adding some of the actual pages from Ray's diaries, but Mr. Roberts informed me that there were many sensitive passages in the diaries and that, believe it or not, most of his writings would probably be redacted because of the new Homeland Security Act.

I was a bit confused at first, but Mr. Roberts explained that it would do no good to inform the "wrong people" of the actual locations of the aqueducts that left the Catskills and meandered downstate to New York City.

I instantly understood what he meant and knew I didn't want to be the one person to allow those who sought to wreak havoc on citizens of the United States an opportunity to stop the flow of clean water to the nation's largest city.

Mr. Roberts did, however, send me pertinent information about the history of the times in which Ray became one of the lead engineers for some of the various Catskill Projects.

In 1905 the New York Board of Water Supply was created by the State Legislature. After careful study, the City decided to develop the Catskill region as an additional water source. The Board of Water Supply proceeded to plan and construct facilities to impound the waters of the Esopus Creek, one of the four watersheds in the Catskills, and to deliver the water throughout the City.

This project, to develop what is known as the Catskill System, included the Ashokan Reservoir and Catskill Aqueduct and was completed in 1915.

It was subsequently turned over to the City's Department of Water Supply, Gas, and Electricity for operation and maintenance.

The remaining development of the Catskill System, involving the construction of the Schoharie Reservoir and Shandaken Tunnel, was completed in 1928.

In 1927 the Board of Water Supply submitted a plan to the Board of Estimate and Apportionment for the development of the upper portion of the Rondout watershed and tributaries of the Delaware River within the State of New York. This project was approved in 1928. Work was subsequently delayed by an action brought by the State of New Jersey in the Supreme Court of the United States to enjoin the City and State of New York from using the waters of any Delaware River tributary.

In May of 1931, the Supreme Court of the United States upheld the right of the City to augment its water supply from the headwaters of the Delaware River. Construction of the Delaware System was begun in March 1937.

THE LAFAYETTE EXPERIENCE - 2011

Fifteen years after my first visit to Lafayette, I was invited by Mr. Joe Micon, a former Democratic member of the Indiana House of Representatives, to attend the naming of the Lafayette Urban Ministries (LUM) Youth Center. During my two-day visit, I was impressed with the schedule that Joe had set up for me.

On August 18th, I sat for an hour-long interview in the studios of Purdue's NPR affiliate radio station, WBAA, visited Ray's fraternity, Sigma Nu, and then shuffled off to the annual Purdue football kick-off banquet where I was afforded a table to display many items of Ray's memorabilia.

Mixing historic track & field memorabilia with the frenzied Purdue football fans might have been a bad idea, but Joe Micon proved to me that all campus sports, new and old, are revered and respected as proved by the many students and athletes who stopped by to inspect Ray's cache.

Joe and I started out early the next day by attending a prayer breakfast with members of the Lafayette Urban Ministries before attending the actual naming ceremony at the Youth Center. After engaging with the staff and the happy children who were part of the ceremony, all of us went outside.

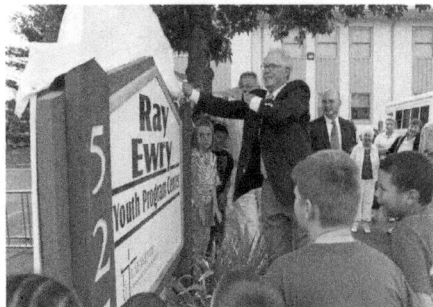

We gathered around a large structure draped in white cloth on the front lawn of LUM and waited for the kids to settle.

Once the reporters and cameramen were in position, Joe gave me the sign and I removed the cloth to reveal the sign with Ray's name on it. It was then that I realized Ray meant more to the citizens of Lafayette than just being a local hero from way back.

It was quite moving to see the faces of the children who would benefit from the love and compassion from the members of LUM.

Once the ceremony was completed, I met the gracious members of the Historic Centennial Neighborhood Association, and finally, moving on to the Purdue campus, Joe and I had a meeting with track & field offices where I met Coach Jack Warner at the newly renovated Mackey Arena.

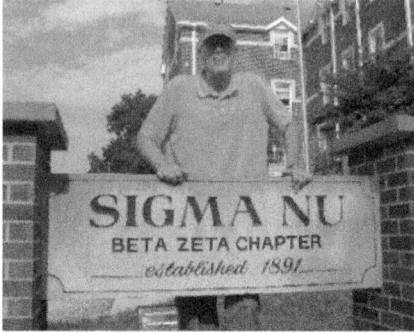

On my final day on campus, I had a few hours before flying back to Baltimore and this gave Joe Micon and me time to visit Ray's fraternity, the Beta Zeta Chapter of the national fraternity, Sigma Nu.

We were introduced to some of the brothers and given a quick tour of their frat house that was being renovated for the new school year.

It was heart-warming to see they had a plaque on the wall that evidenced the Ray C. Ewry Library had been established in the house.

BALTIMORE, MARYLAND - 2012

I received a phone call from Joe Micon informing me that there was a local gentleman, Mr. Dick Leill, who had always been extremely interested in Ray's story and had created a Raymond C. Ewry Memorial committee in hopes of gathering the proper funds to erect a monument to Ray.

I found out later that Mr. Leill had for many decades been an admirer of Ray's life and accomplishments and had been thinking of a way to honor his hometown hero. I was speechless when told that Mr. Leill was planning the building of a granite monument to honor Ray.

When word came back to me that the funds had been raised, a site chosen, Ray's Lafayette Jefferson High School, and a date set, I knew I would be flying back out to Lafayette again.

Once again, Joe Micon and now Dick Leill, who seem to always be looking for avenues to honor Ray, had found another way to bring Ray's name into the present.

Exactly eleven months to the day of the 2011 trip, my oldest son and I were standing in an early morning rainstorm at Spring Vale Cemetery.

Joe Micon and Dr. Cindy Eberts met us at the cemetery and introduced us to Dick and Judy Leill and members of their family. State Representative Sheila J. Klinker and L.A. Clugh, a distant Ewry relative, joined our small entourage as the rain stopped on cue.

A network reporter and a TV cameraman from Indianapolis recorded Mr. Leill's moving dedication to Ray and the laying of 10 yellow roses representing 10 gold medals on Ray's marker.

After the brief ceremony, most of us headed to the LUM Youth Center for another dedication of a massive picture of Ray in his Olympic togs to be hung in the great room of the Center. My son and I were quite moved to see all the children dressed in custom-made T-shirts with Ray's image on them.

Doing our best to stay on time with Joe Micon's schedule, we piled into  cars and headed for Jefferson High School for the first part of the monument's dedication ceremony. The following speakers joined Joe Micon, Dick Leill, and me on stage in the auditorium for numerous accolades to Ray Ewry.

Dr. Jeff Studebaker – Jefferson High School principal

Tony Roswarski – Mayor of Lafayette

John Dennis – Mayor of West Lafayette

Calvin Williams – Assistant Athletic Director – Purdue University

Sheila J. Klinker – State Representative

Ron Alting – Indiana State Senator

Susan Broullette – Assistant to State Senator Richard Lugar

Brian & Randy Allen – Ewry monument builders

After the indoor ceremony, we all headed outside to the track where we came across this six-foot-high covered structure. The high school band was there along with dozens of spectators and the honored speakers as Dick Leill presented the monument.

My son and I stood in anticipation as the covering was pulled off to reveal this simply stunning monument to Ray.

Tears welled in our eyes as the applause rippled around us and we witnessed something we would have never thought possible even a few months before.

Thanks to Dick Leill, Joe Micon, Dr. Eberts, government officials, and all the fabulous people on the monument committee, Ray's legacy was not just confined to sports history books or a plaque on the walls of private athletic clubs depicting his history.

THE SIGMA NU HISTORICAL CONNECTION – 2013

After yet another re-write of "UNSUNG", I felt there wasn't too much I had missed when compiling as much information relevant to Ray's story. I realized that there might always be more out there, but time demanded I finish the book.

About a week before sending what I believed to be the finished product to my editor, I received a phone call from Mr. Bob McCully who introduced himself as the Grand Historian of Sigma Nu. He told me that he was writing an article about Ray and asked if I could add some anecdotes.

I was happy to do so, and we had a wonderful phone interview that would be injected into his article in the "*DELTA*", the fraternity's national magazine.

He also told me he would be visiting the fraternity's national headquarters in Lexington, Virginia, and while on the east coast, he would like to come to Baltimore and have a face-to-face.

His visit was short but sweet and as I waved goodbye, I knew I had met a true professional and a dedicated man whom the members of Sigma Nu must know is an important part of recording Sigma Nu's long and proud legacy.

After Bob left Baltimore, I remembered that I wanted to know what year Ray was inducted into Sigma Nu, so I called him. He said he would do some quick research and get back to me. A week later, I found a postal box from Bob on my front porch.

Too curious for words, I ripped the box open to find the authentic application form for Sigma Nu. Ray had filled out the form on September 26, 1896, as the 51st initiate to be accepted.

Once again, a total stranger has come out of the shadows with pertinent information about Ray. To Bob McCully, I extend my utmost thanks for adding a very important missing piece to the puzzle that is Ray Ewry's life.

53

THE RAY EWRY HIGHWAY – Lafayette, Indiana - 2014

By this time, I knew that Ray's story was a never-ending one that continues to build with each disclosure of his past or additional accolades added to his legacy.

Once again, Dick Leill's tenacity surfaced when he called me and informed me that he had pulled some strings and convinced a bevy of people to name a highway after the Olympian. He might be in his senior years, but Dick is undaunted when it comes to Ray Ewry.

He might not want to take credit for it, but out of the blue comes this amazing AP press release.

Lafayette-born Olympian may get his name on a highway

Tom Carson (grandson) attending

Associated Press

LAFAYETTE – A Lafayette native who overcame childhood trauma and illness to win 10 Olympic gold medals in the early 20th century could soon have part of a state highway named after him.

A resolution authored by state Sen. Brandt Hershman and passed last week by the Indiana Senate urges the Indiana Department of Transportation to rename a section of U.S. 231 the "Ray Ewry Memorial Highway."

Ewry was orphaned when he was 5 years old and then stricken two years later with infantile paralysis and rheumatic fever, the Journal & Courier reported.

Doctors predicted he would spend his life in a wheelchair. But Ewry overcame the illness and went on to win 10 gold medals for standing high jump, standing broad jump, and standing triple jump during the Olympics from 1900 to 1908.

The resolution passed the Senate in the session's final days and was not considered in the House. But Hershman, R-Buck Creek, said he's hopeful INDOT will be able to act with the approval of only one chamber of the General Assembly.

Ewry, who died in 1937, is now little-known for his accomplishments. A granite monument bearing his likeness and a description of his inspiring life story was dedicated in 2012 at Jefferson High School, thanks to the efforts of Buck Creek resident Dick Leill.

Leill said he would be thrilled if Ewry's name could be placed on the new U.S. 231 from River Road to U.S. 52 West.

"He was just as outstanding an academic as he was an athlete," Leill told the Journal & Courier. "He was the lead engineer on the aqueduct project that brought drinking water to New York City and is still used today."

Hershman said he introduced the resolution after Leill contacted him and recounted Ewry's story.

Pictured left to right at the Ray Ewry Memorial Highway Presentation:

Thomas E. Carson, Dick Leill, Joe Micon

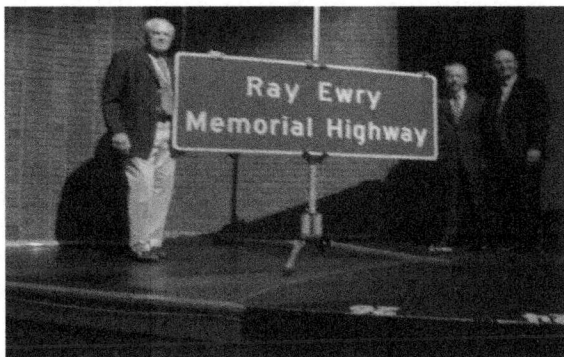

After the naming of the highway, I couldn't think of anything else anyone could do regarding Ray's legacy in Lafayette, but Dick Leill came into the picture again.

He informed me that since Ray was a man of numbers...in his university career at Purdue as a mechanical engineering student, his career with the U.S. Navy in New Jersey, his amazing career representing the USA in four Olympics, and finally his long, successful career as an engineer for the State of New York while acting as a judge for hundreds of track & field events...he simply couldn't abide with a long-ago mistake.

The artisan who carved Ray's headstone made the mistake with the birth year. During the many times I visited Ray's gravesite I always noticed the incorrect year and knew it should have been 1873 but didn't let it get to me.

But, alas, it did get to Dick Leill.

Dick called me a few months ago and said he just couldn't let the mistake go since Ray was a man of numbers and it would be proper to have his headstone changed to the correct year. He has arranged for a stonemason to grind down the face of the stone and etch in the proper years.

I honestly don't know if I can thank Dick enough for the many amazing actions and tributes Dick and Judy Leill have added to Ray's legacy, but I and my family consider Joe Micon, Dick and Judy Leill, and Dr. Eberts part of our extended Olympic family out there in Lafayette, Indiana.

ACKNOWLEDGEMENTS

Before I begin the final section of this book, I must first express my total respect, admiration and thanks to all the writers and researchers from around the world who have documented and written about the Olympic Games since 1896. Without their dedication to their craft, much of what is known of the Games would be mere hearsay.

While researching for this book, I had the help of many experts, both living and now deceased, whose efforts took longer than I have years left on this planet. The following people have changed my life by assisting in my research and opening avenues of discovery, so I could complete my search for amazing things to happen with Ray Ewry's legacy.

Jim and Margaret McKay – Monkton, Maryland

I need to recognize the man who was the voice of the Olympics and his gracious wife for convincing me to write about Ray. It was Jim who sat me down and made me promise to bring Ray's inspirational story to life. He was a source of constant support during the early stages of writing this book. I'm sure I speak for the entire sports and broadcasting community when I say that he is sorely missed.

Cindelyn Eberts, Ph.D. – Author, Researcher

Special thanks to Dr. Eberts for her dedicated research on Ray Ewry. No one I have met in all the years of working on this project has gone to such lengths in probing deep into the rich history of Lafayette and the Ewry and Elisha families.

Her tenacity for the facts has taught me that if you want the correct information on an historical person, you must forget how much time it might take…just keep digging.

Cindy was the only person to discover Ray's birthplace on 4th Street and the fact that Ray's and Nelle's ashes had indeed been transferred to their final resting place back home in the Springvale Cemetery in Lafayette, Indiana.

Alameda McCullough – Lafayette, Indiana

Mrs. McCullough, the curator of the Tippecanoe Historical Society, was instrumental in providing pertinent information about early Lafayette and putting me in contact with people and historical facts that helped me compile early information for this book.

Purdue University – West Lafayette, Indiana

To my initial contact, Mr. Jim Vruggink and Mr. Morgan Burke of the Purdue Athletic Department, and the many contributors to the eArchives website of Purdue University, I give many thanks for their kindness and assistance during my visits to Purdue and the induction of Ray Ewry to the first class of the Purdue Sports Hall of Fame. I also need to thank Track & Field Coach Jack Warner who took time out of his busy schedule to spend time with me.

Sydney Thayer - Cappy Productions[19] – New York City

As described in an earlier chapter, I met Sydney in the early 1980s and I find it fitting that Sydney is included in my list of valued supporters of my project.

I wish to thank him for taking time out of his heavy production schedule while working for the greatest Olympic documentarian on the planet, Mr. Bud Greenspan, to assist me in searching for any archival film footage of Ray.

---

[19] Jonah J. "Bud" Greenspan (September 18, 1926 – December 25, 2010) was a film director, writer, and producer known for his Olympic and various sports documentaries at Cappy-Petrash Productions.

Sydney was also instrumental in directing me to Dr. Bill Mallon and June Becht in the early days of my research. My journey could not have happened without his input and constant support.

Eric Simon – Getty Images – New York City

Special thanks must go out to Eric Simon for digging into the Getty Images archives and discovering the only known video clip of Ray while competing in the 1908 London Olympics for the standing high jump.

Searching for any footage of Ray was the first step on the road to discovery and after all the years of letter writing and phone calls around the world, Eric Simon came up with the only known footage of Ray. I thank him for his time and contribution to the project.

The Ewry family of Marin County, California

Throughout this wonderful journey into Ray's life and times, I have had the distinct pleasure of making new friends, establishing new contacts, and even discovering previously unknown Ewry relatives.

While searching for any press articles on Ray, I came across an article on the *marinij.com* website written by Barry Spitz. It focused on a young lady named Madeline Ewry from Marin County, California who was a track star at Redwood High School.

I wanted to introduce myself to the Ewry's of California and sent an e-mail to Mr. Spitz asking if there was any way he could forward my contact numbers to the family. Instead, he wrote back with the exact phone numbers I needed.

I called and spoke to Madeline's mother, Wendy, who told me about her daughter's track career and went on to fill me in on the whole Ewry clan out there. The next morning, I was introduced to Madeline's grandparents, Ed and Carole Ewry.

Rebecca Jenkins – Author - Durham, England

When I saw Ms. Jenkins' book, *"The First London Olympics - 1908"*, on the Barnes & Noble website, I ordered it immediately. I read it twice before I had the thought of looking her up on the Internet and found she had her own web page.

I wrote an e-mail to her expressing my thanks for her tireless research and great storytelling of the Games of 1908 London. She wrote me back and offered to assist me with any research problems I might come across.

Later, after finding out that she had the original drawing of Ray by the artist, Torsten Schonberg, I asked her permission to reproduce the drawing for my project.

She informed me that it was public domain and graciously gave me best wishes for the success of the project, so special thanks go to Ms. Jenkins for being so cordial and informative. I can only hope to achieve the level of professionalism and talent that she displays.

William James Mallon, M.D. – Durham, North Carolina

I have mentioned Dr. Mallon throughout this book as the "go-to" authority on all things Olympic. I thought that the readers might wish to see why I, and anyone on the planet, would refer to his body of work.

DR. MALLON'S ACCOMPLISHMENTS - PUBLICATIONS

Professional golfer (retired)

Orthopedic surgeon in Durham, North Carolina

Co-founder/past president of the International Society of Olympic Historians

Historical consultant for organizing committees for Atlanta and Sydney Olympics Awarded the Olympic Order medal for services to the Olympic movement (2001)

Dr. Mallon's Publications on Olympics

Quest for Gold. Leisure Press New York City 1984 ISBN 0-88011-217-4 (with Ian Buchanan)

The Olympic Record Book. ISBN 0-82402-948-8, **Taylor & Francis** 1988

Who's Who der Olympischen Spiele 1896-1992. ISBN 3-928562-47-9, Agon-Sportverlag Kassel 1992 (with Erich Kamper)

Historical Dictionary of the Olympic Movement. ISBN 0- 81083-062-0, Scarecrow Press 1996 (with Ian Buchanan)

The 1896 Olympic Games: Results for All Competitors in All Events. With Commentary. ISBN 0-78640-379-9, McFarland & Company, Jefferson (North Carolina) 1997, (with Ture Widlund)

The 1900 Olympic Games: Results for All Competitors in All Events. With Commentary. ISBN 0-78640-378-0, McFarland & Company, Jefferson (North Carolina) 1997.

The 1904 Olympic Games: Results for All Competitors in All Events. With Commentary. ISBN 0-78640-550-3. McFarland & Company, Jefferson (North Carolina) 1999.

The 1906 Olympic Games: Results for All Competitors in All Events. With Commentary. ISBN 0-78640-551-1, McFarland & Company, Jefferson (North Carolina) 1999.

The 1908 Olympic Games: Results for All Competitors in All Events. With Commentary. ISBN 0-78640-598-8, McFarland & Company, Jefferson (North Carolina) 2000. (with Ian Buchanan)

The 1912 Olympic Games: Results for All Competitors in All Events. With Commentary. ISBN 0-78641-047-7, McFarland & Company, Jefferson (North Carolina) 2001. (with Ture Widlund)

The 1920 Olympic Games: Results for All Competitors in All Events. With Commentary. ISBN 0-78641-280-1, McFarland & Company, Jefferson (North Carolina) 2003. (with Anthony Bijkerk)

VALIDITY OF THE 1906 ATHENS OLYMPICS

Since beginning this project, I have been somewhat confused and curious about the opinion of the I.O.C. regarding the validity of the 1906 Athens Olympics, known as "The Intercalated Olympics".

I did some research, possibly for selfish reasons, and found that I was not the only person to take issue with their decision. I have added some opinions from others about this issue and am pleased to enter them into the argument.

"Today, the IOC and a few sports historians do not consider the 1906 Intercalated Olympics to be "true" Olympic Games. By doing so, they not only neglect the Games that may have helped save the Olympic Movement, but we also think it is historically incorrect. After the debacles of 1900 and 1904, the Olympics were in desperate straits. The Greeks had wanted to host more Olympics and they proposed holding "interim" Olympics, every four years in between the Olympics. The first of these was scheduled in 1906.

"These Games were also the first to have all athlete registration go through the N.O.C.'s. They were the first to have the opening ceremony of the Games as a separate event; an event at which for the first time the athletes marched into the stadium in national teams, each following its national flag. They also introduced the closing ceremony and the raising of national flags for the gold, silver, and bronze medal winners."

"The 1906 Games were quite successful. Unlike the 1900, 1904, or 1908 Games, they were neither stretched out over months nor overshadowed by an international exhibition. Their crisp format was most likely instrumental in the continued existence of the Games."

Sports Reference, LLC website

In response to the question of why the I.O.C. regards the 1906 Olympic Games as "unofficial", Dr. Bill Mallon responded in a letter to me.

We did have a committee that spoke to the IOC back in 2006 and tried to get them to change their view on the 1906 Olympic Games. It did not work. We wrote up a policy statement, which I will try to send you as well. Not certain they are going to make the change on this, which should be obvious.

At the 41st Session of the IOC in London in 1948, Dr. Ferenc Mező, a Hungarian member, proposed that the Intermediate Games in Athens (1906) should be accepted as the III Olympic Games. It was decided that this proposal would be placed in the hands of the Brundage Commission.

The Brundage Commission was a three-man commission headed by future IOC President Avery Brundage (USA). The other members were Sidney Dawes (CAN) and Miguel Angel Moenck (CUB). They met in New Orleans, Louisiana in January 1949.

In their report, the Brundage Commission noted, "It is not considered that any special recognition that the IOC might to participants in these Games at this late date would add any prestige, and the danger of establishing an embarrassing precedent would more than offset any advantage. They presented their report at the 42nd Session in Rome in 1949.

Their report dealt with 32 items, the 4th of which was the 1906 Olympic Games. The item was listed as "Acceptance of the Intermediate Games 1906," and the Brundage Commission conclusion was "Rejected."

As stated, a few historians do not consider them to be the Olympic Games, most notable Olympic historians do. The International Society of Olympic Historians has sought official recognition for these Games, but this has not been granted by the IOC.

We support the thesis of those who consider the 1906 Intercalated Games as the Olympic Games and have included all events and competitors in our database.

Bill Mallon, M.D.

Whether a change of heart by the International Olympic Committee will ever take place regarding their opinion of the official status of the 1906 Athens Olympics will always be a point of conjecture.

My respect for Dr. Mallon and his group to challenge the I.O.C. on their decision in the matter of the 1906 Olympics being made official knows no bounds.

There seems to be an ever-increasing groundswell of support to make those Games official and I am notifying each person and organization that wants to carry on the crusade for reconsideration has my utmost support. What's right is right, and if most organizers, athletes, and most of the world recognize the 1906 Olympic Games as legitimate, as the United States Olympic Committee does, then let's band together once and for all and do what's right.

Those Olympians and all who came before and after them deserve to have their efforts and their records honored and placed into the record books.

New York Athletic Club

When I first contacted their offices in 1980, the officials seemed eager to make proper restitution for the theft of Ray's Olympic gold medals. To their credit, two copies of Ray's medals were reproduced and mailed to me along with Ray's original A.A.U. medals and his NYAC medals and trophies. Unfortunately, the remaining eight stolen medals have never been reproduced and I have never been given a reason why.

The promises made by Mr. Willman and Mr. Reddington have only been partially kept. I have made inquiries regarding the existence of an official police report and found that the NYAC never reported the theft and there is no evidence of a police report. I also was somewhat disappointed that there was no evidence of insurance coverage on Ray's stolen medals.

Regarding these two disclosures, I must ask, "why not?"

One might think that an organization as prestigious as the New York Athletic Club would be concerned about its responsibility to its history and members, especially to one who was inducted into its own Hall of Fame and featured on the cover of the March 2012 edition of the "Winged Foot", the NYAC's official Club magazine.

Authors

I wish to thank Dr. Lucas of the University of Pennsylvania and the author of the first Olympic reference book I ever read.

To Mr. David Wallechinsky, who wrote *"The Complete Book of the Olympics;* and to Mr. C. Robert Paul, author of *"The Olympic Games".*

To the exceptional writer and researcher from St. Louis, Mrs. June Becht, who helped me begin my research by pointing me in the right direction.

Another book that should be on the list of anyone interested in reading about the 1904 St. Louis Games is by George R. Matthews who wrote *"America's First Olympics; The St. Louis Games of 1904".*

Special thanks and praise should be afforded to Mr. Fred G. Jarvis for his incomparable book, "From Vision to Victory".

RAYMOND C. EWRY ACCOMPLISHMENTS

- Engineering consultant to the Sanitary Commission at the

  Hudson-Fulton Celebration
- Instructor in Mechanism at the Platt Institute, Brooklyn, New York
- New York Department of Water Supply

AMATEUR ATHLETIC UNION OF THE UNITED STATES

1897 - A.A.U. – Standing High Jump – Gold

1898 - A.A.U. – Standing High Jump – Gold

1899 - A.A.U. – Standing Broad Jump – Gold

1901 - A.A.U. – Standing Broad Jump – Gold

1906 - A.A.U. – Standing Triple Jump – Silver

1906 - A.A.U. – Standing High Jump – Gold

1906 - A.A.U. – Standing Broad Jump – Gold

1907 - A.A.U. – Three Standing Jumps – Gold

1907 - A.A.U. – Standing Broad Jump – Gold

1909 - A.A.U. – Standing Broad Jump – Gold

1909 - A.A.U. – Three Standing Jumps – Gold

1910 - A.A.U. – Three Standing Jumps – Gold

1910 - A.A.U. – Standing Broad Jump – Gold

Holder of World Records in standing high, broad and triple jumps

Twenty-Eight National and Metropolitan first-place finishes

NEW YORK ATHLETIC CLUB

1904 - Standing Broad Jump – Gold

1905 - Standing Broad Jump – Gold

1905 - Standing High Jump – Gold

1906 - Standing High Jump – Gold

1906 - Standing Broad Jump – Gold

1907 - Standing Broad Jump – Gold

1908 - Standing Broad Jump – Gold

OLYMPIC GAMES

1900 Paris – 3 Gold Medals

1904 St. Louis – 3 Gold Medals

1906 Athens – 2 Gold Medals [20]

1908 London – 2 Gold Medals

Ray Ewry established Olympic records in the standing high, broad and triple jumps.

---

[20] Declared unofficial by the I.O.C. but official by everyone else

POST-OLYMPIC AFFILIATIONS

Chief Engineer for completion of the U.S. cruiser "Chattanooga"

Chief Engineer for completion of the U.S. torpedo boats "Nicholson" and "O'Brien"

Engineering consultant to the Sanitary Commission at the Hudson-Fulton Celebration

Chief Engineer for steam work on the new battleship "New York"

Instructor in Mechanism at the Platt Institute, Brooklyn, New York

New York Department of Water Supply

MEMBER OF THE FOLLOWING ORGANIZATIONS

American Society of Naval Engineers

Purdue Alumni Association of New York

New York Alumni Chapter of Sigma Nu

Indiana Society of New York

New York Athletic Club

HONORS

New York Athletic Club Hall of Fame

Purdue Athletic Hall of Fame

United States Track & Field Hall of Fame

United States Olympic Hall of Fame - 1983

International Olympic Hall of Fame

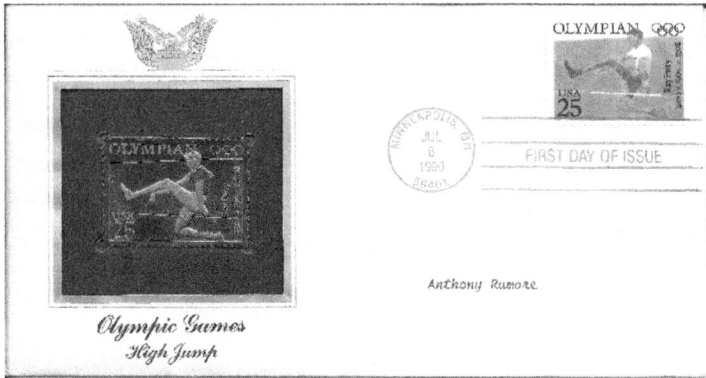

POSTSCRIPT

The Olympics have been an integral part of my life since I was old enough to understand what my mother told me about her father's life. It's an institution reincarnated by the dream of one man, Baron de Coubertin. His dream has allowed the dreams of thousands of dedicated athletes from around the world to come true by being able to compete on the largest stage in the world of sports.

As stated earlier, I wanted to keep my promise to my mother to open the private family archives to all who might wish to know more about Ray Ewry's life and times. It is with great humility that I offer to you what I feel is pertinent to the project.

My ultimate wish is that Raymond Clarence Ewry will no longer be an "UNSUNG" hero of the early Olympics, but an example not just for Olympians, but for everyone who must challenge themselves to be the best they can be no matter what adversities they encounter.

For all future Olympians, I wish you the best of luck in your journey to greatness and hope you recognize those who came before you. They passed the torch along in the hope that you honor the universal creed, *"Citius, Altius, Fortius"*!

Thomas E. Carson, V
Baltimore, Maryland

NOTE FROM THE AUTHOR

To keep the reader's costs down, the author decided to display the photographs and documents taken from Ray Ewry's archives in black and white.

Should the reader wish to view more black & white and color photographs along with legacy documents that grace this biography, please visit the **Facebook** page entitled **RAYMOND C. EWRY**.

If anyone wishes to contact the author regarding more information on Ray Ewry, please feel free to contact:

Thomas E. Carson

ray.ewry.research.group@gmail.com

carson.survivor17@gmail.com

INDEX

Made in United States
Orlando, FL
06 May 2022